CW00828326

NOW
IS THE
TIME

*The voice of one crying in the wilderness,
prepare ye the way of the Lord*

Theresa Holder

ISBN 979-8-89043-565-1 (paperback)
ISBN 979-8-89043-566-8 (digital)

Copyright © 2024 by Theresa Holder

All rights reserved. No part of this publication may be reproduced, distributed, or transmitted in any form or by any means, including photocopying, recording, or other electronic or mechanical methods without the prior written permission of the publisher. For permission requests, solicit the publisher via the address below.

Christian Faith Publishing
832 Park Avenue
Meadville, PA 16335
www.christianfaithpublishing.com

Printed in the United States of America

CONTENTS

NOW IS THE TIME

I know now is the time for God's people to raise up and take their place.

While some people will find a few of the ideas put forth in this book controversial, I hope you will be stimulated to do your own research and to consider the points made. And of the parts of which there is very little research to be found, being mindful that just as they are now changing facts right in front of our faces, they have certainly done away with a lot of the information that at one time was known and acceptable truth.

We will start with the beginning as we know it to be recorded in the Bible, looking at it in a new way. The following paragraph is from the Hebrew text.

We will be looking at time in several different ways. First one is the creation: "In the beginning created Elohiym the heavens and the earth." We are told in Genesis 1:2 that "the earth was without form and void and darkness upon face of deep, and wind Elohiym hovering upon face of the waters and said, Elohiym, there shall be light and there was light and saw, Elohiym, the light that good and divided Elohiym between the light and between the darkness and called Elohiym the light Day and the darkness He called Night and there was evening and there was morning day one" (Hebrew word for word).

These words *Day* and *Night* are capitalized in the Bible because they are not just the day and night spoken of in the rest of the chapter; this light was God's light brought into the darkness of Satan's kingdom. He divided the light, God's kingdom, and darkness, separating the two kingdoms. God called his kingdom Day, and he called Satan's kingdom Night. God brought his light and said, "Light in me be."

John 1:3–4 says, "In Him was life and the life was the light of men and the light shineth in darkness and the darkness comprehended it not."

Second Peter 3:8 tells us to "be not ignorant of this one thing, that one day is with the Lord as a thousand years, and a thousand years as one day." This being true, let us consider that God took seven thousand years in the recreation of the earth. This is not unbiblical; although for reasons beyond me, few consider it. Thinking that the light and darkness spoken of in verses 2 to 13 are the lights we know now, the twenty-four-hour day, this seems unlikely as they were not created until day four. God was also creating time with each day, pronouncing evening and morning day one, evening and morning day two, and so on through day six. But the seventh day, he did not pronounce evening and morning; he only blessed it. God created time as he created or rather recreated the earth. Time is a dimension to house sin as one-third of his creation, the angels. His supernatural Sons had already rebelled. And time will end in Revelation 10:6. We find an angel swearing by him that liveth for ever and ever, who created heaven and earth, and all things that are therein, that there should be time no longer.

For an increased understanding of the Genesis creation story and the flood story, I recommend a small book called *The Marvel of Earth's Canopies* by Professor C. Theodore

Schwarze, published by Good News Publishers, copyright 1957.

The time between Genesis 1:1 and 1:2 is not known, but we do know that in God is no darkness at all, only light. So we know something very bad had happened to his beautiful Eden. This planet, it appears, was the area God had given to a very beautiful angel, son of God, named Lucifer, meaning brightness. He is also called son of the morning, or the light. He reflected the light of God. And since he was the one the other creations saw, he might have begun to think that light was him. Much like we do if we confuse the light in us with ourselves and not give the glory to God. This is called the mystery of iniquity that works in the world until he who now letteth (hold down, retain) will let, until he be taken out of the way (2 Thessalonians 2:7). Knowing this, let us speak of ages. They are made up of approximately two thousand years. The first age was the age of Taurus, the bull, known as the Adamic age. The second was the age of Aries, the ram, known as the Abrahamic age. The third was the age of Pisces, known as the church age. These make up the first six thousand years of the history of the earth as we know it. When speaking to Abraham concerning his children going into the land they would inherit, he was told, in the fourth generation, needing the fullness of time to fill up the cup of the Amorites (Genesis 15:16). And when Jesus was born, we are told, when the fulness of time was come, God sent forth his Son (Galatians 4:4). Each age has its own place in the earth's history and had a certain thing that was to happen to usher in the age. We have now entered the seventh day, the age of Aquarius or the millennial, the day of the Lord, where he shall reign a thousand years here on earth.

Concerning the rebellion of the angels, the Bible tells in Ezekiel 28:2–3, 12–13, speaking to the Prince of Tyrus (to cover over). Thus says the Lord (Adonay) God (Yehovah), "Because thy heart is lifted up, and thou hast said, I am a God (El), I sit in the seat if God (Elohim), in the midst of the seas; yet thou art a man, and not God (El) though thou set thine heart as the heart of God (Elohim). Behold thou art wiser than Daniel there is no secret that they can hide from thee. Thou sealest up the sum, full of wisdom and perfect in beauty. Thou hast been in Eden the garden of God."

Lucifer wanted to be as the Most High God (Elyown) (Isaiah 14:14), being a small god was not sufficient for him; he wanted to be as God (Elyown). And to do this, he needed to create life, so I suspect he blew up this planet, experimenting with the atom. I believe he arranged to be off planet when the experiment went down, leaving Baal, Moloch, Ashtaroth, and other angelic beings on the earth at that time, holding the bag. I say this because we find him in the assembly of the sons of God in Job 2:1, "Again there was a day when the sons of God came to present themselves before the Lord, and Satan came also among them to present himself before the Lord." He is also found in the heavens at other times in the Bible.

He is again attempting to discover the secrets of God with CERN. The large hadron collider is trying to find the God particle and the birth of the universe or the big bang, as they call it. If he continues, he just might find the big bang again or make it again.

I ask God what happened to Ashtaroth, as all we hear about him early in the Bible is only a place called Ashtaroth, east of Jordan, in Bashan. He told me, he became Ashtoreth, the goddess of the Phoenicians, that he was also called Astarte. He was also Isis in Egypt, Ishtar to the Babylonians. The Greek identified him/her as Aphrodite. All known as goddess of fertility, beauty, and love, the Romans had a god called Libertus, from which our Statue of Liberty is patterned. It is my opinion that he is still associated with the statue. He is also, as the deity of Ashtaroth received much attention as a character in games, played by many gamers all over the world but especially here un the USA. No wonder, we are having issues with gender fluency.

I looked this up on the Internet and found that in the occult, they know that he is the same. And when summoned up, he will usually appear as Ashtoreth, as the stink of Ashtaroth is so bad that the smell of burnt, rotten flesh so poignant, one can hardly stand it and must have silver in their nose to live. He enjoys being a goddess because of the admiration and veneration he receives. They also say he is very talkative because he thinks he should not be a demon and that what happened to him was wrong, which leads me to believe, Lucifer deceived his inner circle, leaving them to be blown up. He cares for only himself, not even his angels that serve him and especially not humans.

The bull Moloch or Molech, meaning chief deity, was the chief deity of Moab, east of Jordan. He had been observed by early man and was thought to be a god because of the fire that burned in him. Now spirit is energy, and fire is an expression of that energy. God says, "I will bring forth a fire from the midst of thee. It shall devour thee." We could talk of the burning bush Moses saw or the pillar of fire that was with the children of Israel in the wilderness. Psalm 104:4 and Hebrews 1:7 tell us, he makes his angels spirits and his ministers a flame of fire. Psalm 97:3–5 says, "A fire goeth before him, and burneth up his enemies round about. His lightnings enlightened the world; the earth saw and trembled. The hills melted like wax at the presence of the Lord, at the presence of the Lord of the whole earth." Jeremiah, speaking of Moab, said that "a fire shall come forth out of

Heshbon; and a flame from the midst of Sihon (place of their gods) and shall devour the corner of Moab and the crown of the head of the tumultuous ones" (Jeremiah 48::45). Isaiah, speaking of the spirit, said that "they shall go forth and look upon the carcasses of the men that have transgressed against me for their worm shall not die, neither shall their fire be quenched; and they shall be an abhorring unto all flesh" (Isaiah 66:24 and Mark 9:44, 46, 48). The spirit is eternal and cannot die, so the angels that were here when they blew up the first earth have an enteral flame in them. These are the same bulls that compassed Jesus when he hung on the cross. Psalm 22:12–13 says, "Many bulls have compassed me strong bulls of Bashan have beset me round. They gaped upon me with their mouths, as a ravening and a roaring lion." If you are not saved and have enteral life in God, your spirit also will burn forever and not consume; that is why hell is forever. It is the spirit within, burning like an oil well burning, and does never consume.

You might be asking, How do you know? I will tell you something: I have never told anyone before and would rather not tell you now. Many years ago, around 1970, I was raped by a friend. And during the time in the excitement, the spirit, while repeating "you are mine," exposed himself. His eyes were like a fireplace screen with flames leaping inside, and they sparked and flew out into the room, exposing his bull-head and his large horns. His smell became like burnt, rotten flesh, which took a long time to get rid of.

I do know, and the demons of today are not just the disembodied spirits of the Nephilim before the flood but also the disembodied spirits of the first creation. That is why the Bible speaks of the things in heaven in earth and under the earth (Revelation 5:3, 13). The same reason God told Adam and Eve to subdue the earth, there would have been no need to subdue if there was not something out there, outside the garden. These disembodied spirits of the first creation, not the angels, are looking for bodies to inhabit, and they do not look like any creature of this creation. Maybe I'll tell you how I know this later.

Homosexuality and transgender are just when a male demon wants to reside in a female body or a female demon wants to take a male body. These can be dealt with easily if the person involved desires to be free, but there are some that enter inter-uterus. These are intertwined in the person's DNA, and in my opinion, God will need to do the separation. Hebrews 4:12 tells us, "For the word of God is quick and powerful, and sharper than any two-edged sword, piercing even to the dividing asunder of soul and spirit, and of the joints and marrow, and is a discerner of the thoughts and intents of the heart." God is well able to do the dividing of the spirit.

In fact, I am not sure I agree with the ones that say demons are the disembodied spirits of the Nephilim before the flood. As they lived in this creation, and they lived as men and died as men, God has prepared a place for them. And of course, they are not the spirits of the angels that came down. Jude 1:6 tells us that "The Angels which kept not their first estate, but left their own habitation, he hath reserved in everlasting chains under darkness unto the judgement of the great day." And 2 Peter 2:4 says, "God spared not the angels that sinned but cast them down to hell, and delivered them into chains of darkness to be reserved unto judgment." The first book of Enoch tells us that there were about two hundred angels that came down on Mount Hermon, leaving their own habitation. And the leader was Azazel. He taught man war and how to mine the earth of its ores and minerals, also precious stones, and to make weapons of war. He led the angels in having sexual relations with the daughters of man. He taught the painting of the eyelids and other such things.

So God spoke the world back into existence, calling all the elements back into place. And then He created man, a new creation, in his image. This is why the elements of the earth are billions of years old, while this creation is new. God's plan all along is to bring this planet back into the kingdom of his dear Son, using his man and woman that he created for himself. Jeremiah 51:20 says, "Thou art my battle ax and weapons of war; with thee will I break in pieces the nations, and with thee will I destroy kingdoms."

> Now, also many nations are gathered against thee, that say, let her be defiled and let our eye look upon Zion. But they know not the thoughts of the Lord, neither understand they, his counsel; for he shall gather them as the sheaves into the floor. Arise and thresh, O daughter of Zion; for I will make your horn iron, and I will make thy hoofs brass; and thou shall beat in pieces many people; and I will consecrate their gain unto the Lord, and their substance unto the Lord of the whole earth. (Micah 4:11–13)

We will speak more about our part in his plan as we go on through this book.

Now, let us look at time coming at it from another way. Revelations 17:9–11 says, "And here is the mind which hath wisdom. The seven heads are seven mountains, on which the woman sitteth. And there are seven kings; five are fallen, and one is, and the other is not yet come and when he cometh he must continue a short space. And the beast that was and is not, even he is the eighth, and is of the seven, and goeth into perdition." At the time, John was writing that Rome was the power and would have been the sixth head. Let us briefly look back at history. Egypt would be the first head. Assyria would be the second head. Babylon would be the third head. Media Persia would be the fourth head. Greece would be the fifth head. Rome being the sixth head. After that, there was a period of about one thousand years, and then the seventh head begins to show itself, the British kingdom.

The four horsemen were given to us as information, what would happen, so we can be prepared, not to scare us. There have been many white horse riders throughout time: Ramses II of Egypt, the Assyrian kings, Alexander the Great, Constantine of Rome, Genghis Khan, Hitler, and Joseph Stalin to name a few. Zechariah 6:6–8 tells us where the horses are. The white horse and the black are in the north country and have quieted my spirit in the north country for a while. The white horse, the conqueror or power, and the black horse, the finances, are in the north. He that has the money has the power. The grisled (Zechariah's word) or red (John's word) horse went toward the south country. John said he was given power to take peace from the earth, that they should kill one another, and there was given unto him a great sword (The sword of Allah). Now the bay horse rides to and fro through the earth, and death and hell are with him—all matter of death, swords, famine, beast of the earth (maybe microbe or microscopic, as in diseases, as well). All these have always been.

Daniel called this fourth beast for Daniel. (He is already in Babylon, at his time.) This beast is different from the other beasts. We see in Revelations that he is like the leopard, spotted. Nimrod, the father of the Assyrians, had the feet of the bear, Media Persia, and his mouth as the mouth of a lion, the iron teeth of Rome, and the dragon give him his power.

Let us look at this seventh beast and how he came into existence. I won't go into too much history, just enough that perhaps you will study for yourself. As to where Mayer Amschel Bauer came from in this book, when we pick him up—he was in Germany. I will just say here that in Revelation, where God addressed the seven churches, he said to two churches in Asia Minor, Turkey today, that they have them, which say they are Jews and are not but are of the synagogue of Satan. The Rothschild name can be traced to the 1500 century. You might want to look in East Europe; it is a Yiddish name, meaning red coat. His father changed it when he came to Germany to Bauer to fit in. Amschel Moses Bauer was born in Frankfurt, Germany, on October 6, 1710. He was a money changer, the son of Moses Kalman Rothschild. His son, Mayer Amschel Bauer, was born on February 23, 1744 (another date is given of September 19, 1743). He also was a money changer, taught by his father. He traded in rare coins, and he gained the trust of the kings and princes of Europe. This trust allowed him to take care of their massive wealth. He created the first international bank. He installed his five sons, taught in the ways of usuary in five other European cities, where he opened banks, giving loans to the wealthy, collecting large interest. He also took the name Rothschild back (which also means child of the rock) and used the red shield as the family logo for all his businesses. His son, Nathan Mayer Rothschild, was sent to England around 1798, where he turned the Bank of England into the most prosperous bank ever. When Wellington met Napoleon at the Battle of Waterloo, Nathan had people planted on the French side to let him know how the battle was going. When he knew that Wellington had won, he sold all his stocks. Everyone was watching him to see what he would do. When he sold, everyone else sold their stock as well. He was then having his puppets buy up the stock at pennies on the pound, unbeknownst to everyone else. When it was over, Nathan Rothschild was the richest man on earth. The man who controls Britain's money controls the British Empire. He said "Give me control of a nation's money supply, and I care not who makes its laws."

In this book, I will only touch on some of the highlights of the history in this story. As seeds falling through the fingers, I hope they fall on good soil and stimulate curiosity.

The city of London was in the hands of Rothschild and the bank of England. The control of the empire king or queen were just ponds. The Arch of Wellington served as the doorway to Buckingham Palace, but the power lies in the city of London under the bankers, the crown jewels and the crown both are kept in the tower of London in the city, and the king or queen gets to wear them on special occasions. The pomp of the monarchy is just to keep the people from understanding the truth. The king or queen goes once a year and bows to the mayor in the city of London, a corporation called the crown, not to be confused with the monarchy.

Rothschild owned the East India Company, which was the engine of nineteenth-century England. This company-controlled India grew opium there and transported it to China, which was a very productive country until they became addicted to the opium. Their many ships controlled the seas and trade. They brought the slaves to the American south so they could get cheap cotton for their textile companies. They controlled the diamond mines in Africa. The greatness of Britain was built by these Bavarians. And today they are still using child slave labor to mine cobalt and lithium in Africa for our smart phones, computers, and electric cars and are using slave labor in China to manufacture the cheap goods we go to the store and buy, to consume upon our lust. Sorry, sometimes the truth is just crass.

The enemy, Satan (his kingdom), working through man, creates a problem, an open door, through which he can do his diabolical works. His motive of operation is to never let anything go to waste, as is also the Lord's. Satan creates the problem and presents what he will present as an answer to the problem. Any wonder China feels justified in dumping fentanyl into America today, and now they, the same powers that got America involved in slavery, wants us, who fought to overthrow it, to feel guilty and pay reparations? The kingdom of darkness is always using man's goodness against him, which is why we need to be as wise as a serpent and harmless as doves. We do not overcome evil with evil but with good.

This company has all but disappeared from history, and its headquarters is now Chatham House, the Royal Institute of International Affairs, opened in 1920 in the city of London. It claims to be an independent policy institute with a mission to provide commentary on world events and offer solutions on global challenges. Really! You can't make this stuff up. Create the problem, and then give us commentary on how to fix the problem. And of course we are listening to the experts.

It was in midseventeen hundreds that Nathan Rothschild met Adam Weishaupt of Bavaria, who converted from Judaism to become a Jesuit priest and then later became an atheist. The two had many interests in common. On May 1, 1776, Weishaupt founded the illuminati, just two months before the United States signed its Declaration of Independence. It was a secret society to oppose superstition and religious influence over public life. It was outlawed, just nine years later, in 1785, when it is thought to have just gone underground. That usually works about like banning alcoholic beverages, did in the USA. It just pushed it underground.

In their group were Karl Marx and Friedrich Engels. They introduced the Communist Manifesto, introducing the belief that the state should rule all things pertaining to man with extreme cruelty if necessary to bring about the order they wanted. They believed the end justified the means. Among their group was also Charles Darwin. His part was in creating a rash explanation for the origin of species. They rewrote the books to show only the history they wanted us to know. They needed to break down the foundation of the old civilization to bring in the new order. They knew the scriptures very well.

> If the foundations be destroyed,
> what can the righteous do? (Psalm 11:3)

The Fabian Society, founded in 1884, whose logo is a wolf in lamb's coat, believed they would need to heat the world in the fire and remold it to their image. The Fabian Society is a British socialist organization, whose purpose is to advance the principles of social democracy and democratic socialism via gradualist and reformist effort in democracies, rather than by revolutionary overthrow. The Fabian Society was also historically related to radicalism, a left-wing liberal tradition.

Vladimir Lenin, Leon Trotsky, and Joseph Stalin were all students of these socialist democratic teachings, bringing the Bolshevik revolution and communism to a broken Russia. Hitler also, a student of Karl Marx's works, brought terror to Germany and all Europe.

Another one in their group was Cecil J. Rhodes, who was so influential that Nathan Rothschild financed his diamond mines in Africa, and the country of Rhodesia was named after him. He funded scholarships to the great universities, known as Rhode Scholars; one of the proud recipients of this is Bill Clinton.

Another group was Freemasonry, traced to the end of the thirteenth century, the oldest fraternal organization. It has three levels——apprentice, fellowcraft, and master mason—thirty-three degrees in all. While the illuminati are nonreligious, the Freemasons are primarily attractive to religious people because of their great work ethic. The square and compose depict a builder square. The G represents geometry, the grand architect of the universe, with thirty-three degrees for the degrees of the earth and the one-third of the angels, which went into rebellion with Lucifer, the latter of which their members are not aware. They do not know who they are serving until they get to the last degrees, and then it is too late to get out. Another piece of information I've been told but cannot find information on is, supposedly, during the crusades, religious wars between the Christians and Muslims, 1096–1291, fought in the Middle East for the control of the Holy Land. The crusaders met a being, part goat and part man, who gave them the pattern for Solomon's temple and the instructions for the Freemasons. Just as God told King David he could build him a house, but he, God, would build him a house, whose builder and maker is God. In 1 Peter 2:5, it says, "You also, as lively stones, are built up, a spiritual house." Just as God is building a temple for himself, so is Lucifer building a temple for himself.

In case you think this could not be true and is just too crazy for you to believe, and it could not be biblical, south and toward the east of the Dead Sea is Mount Seir; this is the land that Esau moved to. He intermarried with the children of Seir, a Horite. And in the end, he took their land, Seir (Satyr: a he-goat, fawn, devil). Horite means cave dweller. Deuteronomy 2:12 says, "The Ho-rims also dwelt in Seir before-time; but the children of Esau succeeded them, when they had destroyed them from before them, and dwelt in their stead." Before, time here is believed to be before the flood. Hum, maybe the cave dweller, survived the flood. Maybe there is a blood line seed. Numbers 24:21 says, "And he looked on the Ken-ties, (children of Cain) and took up his parable, and said, strong is thy dwelling place, and thou puttest thy nest in a rock." What rock? Maybe Petra could be, child of the rock, just something to consider.

Back to our story, when the young colonies had the nerve to stand up to the bankers of Britain, the crown, the British East Indies, having the world's largest army, started the Revolutionary War in April 1775, and soon the rebel colonies were in the fight for their lives. The French joined the colonies in 1778. And by 1781, the Americans had effectively won their independence, although it took another two years for the British to give up. The British bankers did not give up easily and came back to fight the young America in 1812, this being the first time our congress made a declaration of war. History records that it was only divine providence that saved the United States.

A few years later, during the civil war to set the slaves free (which did not sit well with the bankers, who wanted the money they were making using cheap cotton in their new textile factories), President Lincoln needed financing for his army, but he refused to borrow from the bankers. Instead, he created the Lincoln greenbacks. They used their puppet, John Wilkes Booth, a Southern sympathizer, to assassin Lincoln. This was not the first time they had done this. Benedict

Arnold was another of their tools. It was about the banking and who would control the banks in the United States, the East India House, would be the wizard behind the curtain.

What would be needed to take control of the world would be the great wars. Washington understood this as he said, "Shall a few designing men for their own aggrandizement and to glorify their own avarice overset the goodly fabric we have been rearing at the expense of so much time, blood and treasure?"

With the help of JPMorgan and other players, the bankers, which had the control of the finances of Europe and the United States, began to slow down the flow of money to the United States in 1907, which in turn caused business to slow down and created a depression. The answer was to create a national bank, and they wanted it under the control of the international bankers, the very thing that had brought Hamilton and Burr to a duel in July 1804, leading to Hamilton's death.

They still needed control of the money to finance the wars that would be needed to take control of the world, so they secretly met off the coast of Georgia at Jekyll Island, a rich man's retreat, where they crafted the Federal Reserve Act of December 23, 1913. They would need the approval of congress and the signature of a president. They had two years to find the president. They found him at Princeton University, where he was president of the university, Woodrow Wilson. And they placed their man, Edward Mandell House, at Wilson's side to mentor him. They got Taft to run against Roosevelt, splitting the Republican vote, assuring the election of their Liberal Democrat. With Woodrow Wilson in place and doing their bidding, they passed the Federal Reserve Act two days before Christmas, when everyone wanted to get home for Christmas 1913.

Now all that was needed to start a war was a spark. They got that spark when the archduke of Austria was assessed. June 1914, the war was on. The United States did not want to join the war, and Wilson campaigned on not getting the United States in the war. But soon after winning his reelection, the United States joined the war. America needed to borrow money, and borrow it she did from the Federal Reserve Bank. When the war was over, their next effort was a way to keep the peace and stop wars. The idea floated was a fourteen-point plan called the League of Nations, a super government to bridge the gap, a new world order, and Wilson was assigned the task of selling the idea to the United States. Without the United States, there could not be a plan, but Wilson failed. The bankers would not be denied. They regrouped and called for a new plan. There was a rising star in Germany. He was perceived favorably, a socialist, and they thought they could use him. He had formed the Nazi Party, a socialist democratic party. They could fund both sides of the war and get even more rich, but they had not counted on Hitler's ambition. He proved to have bigger dreams than just Germany. His answer was to kill the Jews and get rid of all of them. He recruited Italy and Japan. And in 1941, after being attack by Japan, the United States was in the war. The British, the seventh head, was waning. And after the war, the bankers got their way, and a new peacekeeping organization was born. Out of the seventh head came the eighth, the United Nations, born in 1945 and established in 1949 its military arm, NATO.

We have looked at the progression of time in two ways: (1) the creation timeline and (2) the beast timeline. Now indulge me one more way, the second temple.

When Israel came back into the Holy Land from Babylon to rebuild the temple, the foundation was laid in

536 BC. The work was discontinued in 534 BC. And then, for fourteen years, due to the withstanding of the enemies of Israel, the work on the temple ceased. Then in 520 BC, a new decree came, and the work continued and was completed in 515 BC, making the total number of years to complete the temple seven, God's number of completeness. Now on the day of Pentecost, the Holy Spirit laid the foundation of the church (God's spiritual temple). The work went strong for about two hundred years, then due to the withstanding of the enemies of God, the work for the most part ceased, and the world experienced what is called the dark ages, lasting for about fourteen hundred years. Then with the invention of the printing press and the awaking of many, the church began to be built again. Now continuing another five hundred years would put us at the end of the age of Pisces and at the beginning of the age of Aquarius. You can see, we are at the same spot in time, no matter which way we got here, and there are other ways as well.

When the children of Israel went from Babylon to the land of Israel to rebuild their temple, their priest was Jeshua, who represents Yeshua. And their governor was Zerubbabel (to burn hot against Baal), representing the Holy Spirit. And the prophets were Haggai and Zechariah. In Zechariah 4:6–9, I will paraphrase, "This is the word of the Lord unto Zerubbabel, saying, not by might nor by power but by my spirit, says the Lord of host. Who are you, O great mountain before Zerubbabel? Thou shall become a plain, and he shall bring forth the headstone with shouting, crying grace, grace unto it. The hands of Zerubbabel have laid the foundation of the house. His hands shall also finish it, and you shall know that the Lord of host has sent me unto you."

Now here are some words for you, spiritual Israel.

Being confident of this very thing; that he which hath begun a good work in you will perform it until the day of Jesus Christ. (Philippians 1:6)

For it is God which works in you, both to will and to do His good pleasure. (Philippians 2:13)

For I know whom I have believed and am persuaded that he is able to keep that which I have committed unto him against that day. (2 Timothy 1:12)

The Lord will perfect that which concerns me; thy mercy, O Lord endures forever; forsake not the works of your own hands. (Psalm 138:8)

I will sing of mercy and judgment, unto thee, O Lord, will I sing. (Psalm 101:1)

The Lord is good, a strong hold in the day of trouble; and he knows them that trust in him. (Nahum 1:7)

And then his words in verse 7 say, "Speak grace, cry grace unto the mountain; the mountain shall become a plain and so, shall you bring forth the headstone." One of the things God is about to do is to show us a new expression of his grace, freely you have received freely give.

God is saying, "I will do a new thing in the world, and now is that time which was spoken of by my servants the prophets."

THE KING AND
HIS KINGDOM

John the Baptist preached, "Repent, for the kingdom of heaven is at hand" (Matthew 3:2). He was sent to prepare the way of the Lord (Matthew 3:3, Mark 1:2–3, and Luke 1:6). We are told that this is that which was spoken of by the prophet Isaiah, saying, "The voice of one crying in the wilderness, prepare ye the way of the Lord. Make his paths straight" (Isaiah 40:3). Just as he was sent to prepare the way for Christ's first coming, so are we here to prepare the way for his second coming.

Jesus said in Luke 7:28, "For I say unto you, among those that are born of women there is not a greater prophet than John the Baptist; but he that is least in the kingdom of God is greater than he." And again, in Matthew 11:12, he said, "And from the days of John the Baptist until now the kingdom of heaven suffereth violence, and the violent take it by force."

Let us consider why Jesus used the term *violence.* If there is violence against the kingdom of God, there must be an enemy. Isaiah 14:12–15 says, "How art thou fallen from heaven, O Lucifer, son of the morning, how art thou cut down to the ground, which didst weaken the nations! For thou hast said in thine heart, I will ascend (alah) into heaven, I will exalt my throne above the stars of God; I will sit also upon the mount of the congregation, in the sides of the north (God's mount). I will ascend above the heights of the clouds; I will be like the Most High (Elyown). Yet thou shalt be brought down to hell, to the sides of the pit." Note Lucifer himself is not destroyed until after he is bound for one thousand years. God deals with everyone else (the beast and false prophet and everyone that worshipped the beast and all that had received the mark of the beast were cast into the lake of fire and the remnant was slain with the sword of him that sat upon the horse, whose sword proceeded out of his mouth), then he is loosed and goes out and raises an army of what I believe is his living dead. They come up against God, and then they are destroyed. And Lucifer is cast into the lake of fire (Revelation 19:20, 21).

> Thou hast been in Eden the garden of God; every precious stone was thy covering...the workmanship of thy tabrets and of thy pipes was prepared in thee in the day that thou wast created. Thou art the anointed cherub that covereth, and I have set thee so; thou wast upon the holy mountain of God; thou hast walked up and down in the midst of the stones of fire. Thou wast perfect in thy ways from the day that thou wast created, till iniquity was found in thee. By the multitude of thy merchandise (trade, as peddling) they have filled the midst of thee with violence, and thou has sinned; therefore, I will cast thee as profane out of the mountain of God; and I will destroy

thee, O covering cherub, from the midst
of the stones of fire. (Ezekiel 28:13–16)

You might ask, if Lucifer or Satan is the enemy of God,
then why would not God just destroy his enemy long ago?
Remember that God is a God of love, a just God, and that
he operates within His own laws. Lucifer as covering cherub
in Eden (the earth in its perfect state), went into rebellion
against God, and took one-third of the angels into his rebellion with him. If God had destroyed Lucifer and the one-
third of angels with him, the other angels and other creations would have seen God as being an unjust God, and
they would have been serving him out of fear. Instead, he
embarked upon his plan to bring the earth back unto the
kingdom of God.

The true story of creation and true science come into
perfect agreement. God spoke. God said, "Let there be," "Let
the earth," "Let the waters," etc. God called back into place
all the former elements of the first creation. But when it came
to man, God said, "Let us make man in our image, after our
likeness." So God created man in his own image. "In the
image of God created he him, male and female created he
them." Mankind is the only thing that God created anew.
And he formed man of the dust of the ground and breathed
into his nostrils the breath of life, and man became a living
soul. All the other creation was a recreation. That is why,
its elements are all much older than this creation and why
if you look at the earth, it is plated together in layers, with
fault lines, and not very stable. It was only called back for a
relatively short time, until God would complete his plan of
redemption.

What does the created in our image mean? Yes, we are
three parts, as is the Godhead, but it is much more than that.

There are many things created in three parts. God breathed into man his spirit, and man became a living soul. Remember, in his creation, he said, "Let everything produce after its kind." And man and his other sons, the created angels, are the only creations that have his spirit and can produce after his spirit. We are to produce and be imagers of God's very own spirit. If man had not fallen, things would be a lot different. But since we did fall, we needed to be redeemed.

Before ever mankind had lost the dominion over the earth, God had his plan in place to go and pay the price of redemption.

> The Lamb slain from the foundation of the earth. (Revelation 13:8)

> Then shall the King say unto them on his right hand come, ye blessed of my father, inherit the Kingdom prepared for you from the foundation of the world. (Matthew 25:34)

> Forasmuch as ye know that ye were not redeemed with corruptible things, as silver and gold, from your vain conversation received by tradition from your fathers. But with the precious blood of Christ, as a lamb without blemish and without spot. Who verily was foreordained before the foundation of the world but was manifest in these last times for you. (1 Peter 18–20)

Hebrews 4:3 tells us that the works were finished from the foundation of the world. Revelation 13:8 tells us that all will worship the Antichrist, whose names are not written in the Book of Life of the Lamb, slain from the foundation of the world. Christ had already made the plan and said, "I will go and shed my blood as the price to purchase back the seed of Adam."

> And God said, let us make man in our image, after our likeness; and let them have dominion over the fish of the sea, and over the fowl of the air, and over the cattle, and over all the earth, and over every creeping thing that creeps upon the earth. So, God created man in his own image, in the image of God created he him; male and female created he them. And God blessed them, and God said unto them, be fruitful and multiply and replenish the earth and subdue it; and have dominion over the fish of the sea, and over the fowl of the air, and over every living thing that moves upon the earth. (Genesis 1:26–28)

I wish to submit here that you do not replenish something that was not plenished before and no need to subdue if there was not something outside the garden that needed to be subdued. God gave Lucifer's former dominion to man, which did not go over very well with Lucifer. But God had a plan.

> Out of the mouth of babes and nursing infants you have ordained strength

25

because of your enemies, that you may
silence the enemy and the avenger. (Psalm
8:2 NKJV)

Notice that it is with the mouth that we will still the
enemy. It is when we return God's Word to him that we have
the dominion.

So shall my word be that goes forth
out of my mouth; it shall not return unto
me void, but it shall accomplish what I
please, and it shall prosper in the thing
for which I sent it. (Isaiah 55:11 NKJV)

Psalm 8:5–6 goes on to tell us that man was created
a little lower than the angels and crowned with glory and
honor. And given dominion over the works of God's hands;
thou hast put all things under his feet.

Thou hast put all things in subjection under his feet. For in that he put all
in subjection under him, he left nothing
that is not put under him. But now we
see not yet all things put under him. But
we see Jesus, who was made a little lower
than the angels for the suffering of death,
crowned with glory and honor; that he
by the grace of God should taste death
for every man. For it became him, for
whom are all things, and by whom are all
things, in bringing many sons unto glory,
to make the captain of their salvation
perfect through sufferings. For both he

that sanctifies, and they who are sancti-
fied are all of one; (Spirit) for which cause
he is not ashamed to call them brethren
(family). (Hebrews 2:8–11)

We know that Satan set out to take back his dominion.
God planted the garden of Eden and put man in the garden,
where God would come and visit with man. God had con-
stant communion with his creation. Man had only to obey
God and not eat of the one tree which God said not to eat,
the tree of knowledge of good and evil, which was placed in
the midst of the garden. God was teaching his man, and his
man was to rule the earth under his direction. Satan knew
that if man would disobey God, he would lose his dominion.
So he set out to get his former dominion back.

So he said to the woman, "Hath God said you shall not
eat of every tree of the garden?"

And the woman said unto the serpent, "We may eat of
the fruit of every tree except of the tree which is in the midst
of the garden. God hath said, 'Ye shall not eat of it, neither
shall ye touch it, lest ye die."

Now I have looked long and hard, and I cannot find
anywhere that God commanded man not to touch the fruit
of the tree of knowledge. In fact, if man was to dress the
garden, as God had said, he would have to touch the tree. I
do, however, find in the last chapter of the Bible, Revelation
22:18–19, that we are not to add to or take away from the word
of God. So perhaps we have found the open door through
which Satan was able to temp Adam and Eve. (Either Adam
had added to God's word, or Eve herself added. We don't
know which.) But Satan was able to persuade them that they
would be as God, knowing good and evil. Was that not how
Satan himself fell, trying to be as God? The Bible says, "And

when the woman saw that the tree was good for food and that it was pleasant to the eyes and a tree to be desired to make one wise, she took of the fruit thereof." (She touched it, and nothing happened.) So she took a bite. Eve was first to fall, and her covering of light went inside her. (Go forth, science, and prove that blood is a corrupt form of the same components as light.) And Adam saw, for the first time, a naked woman, "and she gave also unto her husband with her, and he did eat." (The *apple* and *eat* are probably parable, the apple being fruit or fruitful and eat being partake.) Both Adam and Eve were now in a fallen state. And the direct communion man had enjoyed with God was no longer possible. Notice the woman was deceived, but Adam knew what he was doing. He made a choice to disobey God. So also, the second Adam, Christ, made a choice to redeem or buy back, with His own blood, mankind, whom he had created for his own purpose. Just as Adam made a choice to sin, Jesus would choose to pay the price for sin. "For since by man came death, by man came also the resurrection of the dead. For as in Adam all die, even so in Christ shall all be made alive" (1 Corinthians 15:21–22). Man, created a little lower than the angels, was now able to be restored to a position above the angles in the family of God and thereby given the authority that through the Spirit of God, they might take back the dominion of this earth.

Here we speak a little about the serpent being used as the one temping Eve in the garden. The terms *cherubs* and *serpents* were used in the ancient Mesopotamian writing to indicate throne guards. The ancient Mesopotamians would have understood that the serpent was a supernatural rebel. My money is on Azazel.

First Corinthians 15:45–47 tells us that the first Adam was made a living soul; the last Adam was made a quickening spirit. That was not first that was spiritual, but that which is natural; and afterward that which is spiritual. The first man is of the earth, earthy; the second man is the Lord from heaven. Verse 49 says, "And as we have borne the image of the earthy, we shall also *bear the image* of the heavenly." First Peter 3:18 says, "Christ also hath once suffered for sins, the just for the unjust, that he might bring us to God, being put to death in the flesh, but quickened by the Spirit."

Know that the same spirit that raised Christ up will also raise you up and is well able to keep you if you are willing to surrender yourself unto him. Even Christ had to pray, "Not my will but your will, Father, be done." And in the Lord's prayer in Matthew 6:10, Jesus says, "Thy kingdom come. Thy will be done in earth, as it is in heaven." When we pray in earth, in my option, we should personalize it and say in my earth meaning our own lives, for we are just earthen vessels made to carry the life of Christ. Paul said in 2 Corinthians 4:7, "But we have this treasure in earthen vessels; that the excellence of the power may be of God, and not of us." Satan is deceiving the people of the earth again today by telling them that they can attain to this position without the blood of Jesus, that we really are all gods. This is the message of the new age, which actually has a lot of truth in it but does not have *the truth*, without which none of the other truths will last. They are trying to enter the kingdom without the King. The laws of the universe will work for anyone on this earth, who learns how to work them but will not be able to give life everlasting, which is why you can win the whole world and lose your own soul. *Not a wise choice!*

Is the kingdom of God for now, or is it something we get when we go to heaven?

In Matthew 9:35, we find Jesus went about all the cities and villages, teaching and preaching the good news of the kingdom and healing every sickness and every disease among the people. In Matthew 10:5–8, he sent the twelve apostles out, saying, "Go, preach. The kingdom of heaven is at hand, heal the sick, cleanse the lepers, raise the dead, cast out devils; freely you have received, freely give." When Jesus sent out the seventy, he said, "The kingdom of God is come near unto you." In Luke 9:27, Jesus said to his disciples, "But I tell you of a truth, there be some standing here, which shall not taste of death, till they see the kingdom of God." Jesus made the point that now is the kingdom of God with man. In Luke 17:21b, Jesus said, "The kingdom of God is within you." Now, today, if you will hear his voice, is the day to establish the King to his kingdom of your life. One of the intercessions that God has had through me for years is, "Oh, my people, what aileth thee? Is there no king, no king in thee?" Probably, from Micah 4:9, "now, why dost thou cry out aloud? Is there no king in thee? Is thy counsellor perished?"

Jesus showed himself to the disciples several times, eating with them. He showed them his scars. I asked him one time why he keep the scars, knowing that God was well able to take them away. He said, "So my bride doesn't have to bear her scars." When Jesus heals, he also takes away the scars. Of course, they also serve to identify him to those who would not believe when they look upon the wounds that I received in the house of friends, for he came unto his own, and his own received him not.

When the disciples thought he was a ghost, he said, "Touch, handle me, and see a ghost has not flesh and bones." We are also told in another place that we are flesh of his flesh and bone of his bone, so we know that the resurrected body has flesh and bone. In 1 Corinthians 15:50, we are told "that flesh and blood cannot inherit the kingdom of God, neither doth corruption inherit incorruption." We know that the sin nature is passed through the blood, and that is why there had to be a blood sacrifice made for sin because of the avenger, Satan. Satan is the one that required a blood sacrifice. Jesus came and paid that penalty once, for all. When the enemy accuses you in your conscience, just agree in the way with him (Matthew 5:25) and say, "But Christ already paid the penalty of death for my sins. And in any court, I cannot be tried twice for the same crime, that would be double jeopardy." (He is a legalist.)

John 5:45 says," Do not think that I will accuse you to the father; there is one that accuses you, even Moses, (the Law) in which you trust." Galatians 3:17–18, paraphrased, says, "This I say that Abraham's covenant, that was confirmed before God in Christ, the law, which was four hundred and thirty years after, cannot disannul or make void, that it should make the promise of no effect. For if the inheritance be of the law, it is no more of promise. But God gave it to Abraham by promise." Galatians 3:19, paraphrased, says, "Why the law then? It was added because of transgressions, till the seed should come to whom the promise was made, and it was ordained by angels in the hand of a mediator." Verse 20, paraphrased, says, "Now a mediator means more than one side, but God is one." Please understand, God has not changed. God has always been on the side of man. He made a covenant, and he himself is keeping both sides. We are told that he had his plan before the foundations of the world to pay the price for sin and reunite mankind back to God.

The law, by its very nature, gives power to the soul. Because if we manage a little success in keeping it, then the flesh is puffed up, bringing death. But the Spirit gives life, and that is through Jesus Christ. We find out in the first chapter of Hebrews that God, who spoke in times past by the prophets, has spoken unto us in these last day by his Son, whom he appointed heir of all things, by whom also he made all things and upholding all things by the word of his power when he had, by himself, purged our sins and sat down; on the right hand of the Majesty on high. Verses 4 and 5 say, "Being made so much better than the angels, as he hath by inheritance obtained a more excellent name than they. For unto which of the angels said he at any time, *thou are my Son, this day have I begotten thee*? And again, I *will be to him a Father and he shall be to me a Son.*"

Now in John 17, Jesus prays for us saying, "As thou sent me into the world even so, have I also sent them. I pray for them that they may be one as thou Farther, art in me, and I in thee, that they also may be one in us. The glory which you gave me I have given them; that they may be one, even as we are one; I in them, and thou in me, that they may be made whole in one." We know that man was created in God's image and that God is three parts—Father, Son and Holy Spirit—and that the three are one. (Jesus said, "I only say and do the things the Father says and does.") What we need to realize is that man was created in God's image—three parts: spirit, soul, and body. And by Jesus, through the Holy Spirit dwelling in us, we too must become wholly one, our spirit by *his spirit*, ruling soul and body, operating as one with God. "Then the world will know that you have sent me and have loved them as thou hast loved me." My beloved, this cannot happen until we have become one with Christ. Then the body will not be divided. Making Jesus the king of our lives and entering unto his kingdom will truly establish his body as one. He is the hub, and we are all attached by the Holy Spirit to him. And all revolve around him, as the stars of heaven do, not as in this earth where we have so grown accustomed to there being one person above the other, not so in the kingdom of God, but all are equal in him. The very same equality that the world is trying to obtain cannot be attained without ones with God.

Jesus was under the authority of the kingdom of his Father and had been given all authority over the earth and all of the earth's rulers; and that is who we have authority over, not one another. "For who would judge another man's servant," said Jesus, "he will give answer to his own master."

In Luke 7, we find the story of the centurion, Roman soldier, whose servant was sick. And when he heard that Jesus was in the area, he sent the elders of the Jews to ask Jesus to come and heal his servant, and Jesus went with them. When he was not far from the house, the centurion sent friends to him, saying, "Lord, trouble not yourself, for I am not worthy that thou should enter my house but just say the word and my servant shall be healed. I am also a man set under authority, having under me soldiers, and I say, unto one, 'Go,' and he goes, and to another, 'Come,' and he comes, and to a servant, 'Do this,' and he does it. When Jesus heard these things, he marveled at him and turned and said to the people following, "I say unto you, I have not found so great faith, no not in Israel" (verses 6–9). This centurion understood the kingdom and its authority and that Jesus was under the authority of the kingdom of his Father and had been given all authority over the earth and all the earth's rulers. And when he spoke the word, the sickness would have to leave his servant. The disciples did not understand this truth at that time, and even now it would appear, many do not understand the principles of the kingdom of God. They are trying to be under man's authority, instead of God's. When the children of Israel wanted a king, Samuel went to God, and God said, "Give them their request. It is not you they are rejecting, it is me." The people wanted a king after their flesh, not a king after the Spirit, God.

Jesus now, after his death and resurrection, sat down at the right side of the Father until his enemies are his footstool. "Being by the right hand of God exalted and having received of the Father the promise of the Holy Spirit, he hath sent forth this; which, ye now see and hear. David is not ascended into the heavens; but he said himself, the Lord (Yehovah) said unto my Lord, (Adon) sit thou on my right hand, until I make thy enemies thy footstool" (Acts 2:33–35). Jesus has chosen to work through the Holy Spirit in his body to bring his enemies under his feet. The verses "sit thou at my right hand, until I make thine enemies thy footstool" are recorded in the Bible seven times.

> And the god of peace shall bruise
> Satan under your feet shortly. (Romans
> 16:20)

I am weary of people sitting around, waiting for Jesus to do something for them and to them. He has already done his part when he said it is finished at Calvary. He will not do something for you, only through you. He has chosen to work through his man or woman he created. He made us because he wanted to use us and have a relationship with us, not because he needed us. He wants us to become one (*yachad*) with him as he prayed in John 17.

Paul tells us in 2 Corinthians 5:20 that we are ambassadors for Christ. Now, of ambassadors, they represent the kingdom from which they came, and that kingdom supplies all their needs, their land, their homes, and everything to live and operate in the kingdom into which they are sent. And they have complete immunity. If anyone attacks them, it is seen as attacking the country from which they are sent, and all the powers of that country will defend them. We can see why Jesus said in Matthew 6:24–25, "Take no thought for your own needs," and again in Matthew 17:26, "Then are the children free." In Luke 18:7–8, it says, "Avenge not yourself, for it is God who will avenge you; the whole kingdom of God is behind you. So fear not, my little children."

One time, I ask God why the church was not seeing the signs and wonders which he promised to us in the latter days. This is not to say we do not see any of his glory, but we are only experiencing a small amount of what God wants us to have and has promised to us in his covenant. This is the answer I got. He said we are taking his Holy Spirit and using it like a person would use a wrinkle cream and applying it to our flesh to make the flesh look better. (God wants to work from the inside out, not the outside in.) The Holy Spirit does work, and our flesh does look somewhat better. But that is not his desire for us. His desire is that we would die to our flesh and live in the newness of his spirit (an exchanged life), and all his promises are to the new spirit man. Jesus died to exchange places with us. We see that he died in our stead but fail to see that we should allow him to live in our stead. (Jesus must be our King.) He said you call me Lord, Lord but do not the things that I say. It appears that we are not trusting in him, and we still want to have control ourselves. We are still eating from the tree of knowledge. "They that sanctify themselves and purify themselves in the gardens behind one tree in the midst (shall we just say, 'eating that which is unclean' from our own intellect) shall be consumed together; saith the Lord" (Isaiah 66:17). He also calls this walking in the light of your own candle. We are willing to go out into the river of the Holy Spirit just as long as our feet can touch the bottom so we can still have control. But God wants us out in the deep waters, out of our own control, and into his control. For this, we need to repent and turn our lives over to God anew to have him renew us. Paul said in Galatians 4:19, "My little children, of whom I travail in birth again until Christ be formed in you."

I know from experience that God is not concerned about how our flesh looks or feels. If you have ever suffered in the flesh or suffered loss in any way, you will know that our Lord has his mind on the eternal, while we are concerned about the temporal. We need the mind of Christ. We must have our minds renewed. Ephesians 4:23–24 says, "Be renewed in the spirit of your mind...and put on the new man, which after God is created in righteousness and true holiness." We must trust his word to us; he has given us his covenant, two covenants. Here is a twist on the rainbow covenant. He said, "Between you and me I have placed the bow in the clouds." He will never allow us to suffer more than we can bear but will, with the dark clouds and hard rains, place the bow in the sky, which says to us, the Son is with you. "I am with you, and I will never leave you or forsake you," or give you more than you and I together can bear. In Isaiah 54:9–10, the Lord said, "For this is as the waters of Noah unto me; for as I have sworn that the waters of Noah should no more go over the earth; so, have I sworn that I would not be wroth with thee, nor rebuke thee. For the mountains shall depart and the hills be removed; but my kindness shall not depart from thee, neither shall the covenant of my peace be removed, says the Lord that has mercy on thee."

Now for the other covenant, consider our father Abram through which the promise came.

Now the Lord had said unto
Abram, get thee out of thy country, and

from thy kindred, and from thy father's house, unto a land that I will show thee. And I will make of thee a great nation, and I will bless thee, and make thy name great; and thou shall be a blessing. And I will bless them that bless thee, and course him that curses thee; and in thee shall all families of the earth be blessed. (Genesis 12:1–3)

Now we know that Abram went out, not knowing where he was going, and believed the Lord, and it was counted to him for righteousness. But so many times, we want to know the details first and see if what God is asking makes sense to our mind. This is eating from our intellect, the tree of knowledge, our own intellect, which is in our soul, the garden of the Lord. God is still only asking for obedience; he has never changed. God is the same yesterday, today, and forever and ever. And he says, "How can two walk together unless they be agreed?" Now if he changes not, guess who must do the changing? When we believe and trust God enough to obey him, he counts that as righteousness. So then, righteousness is faith in God and his Word.

For we walk by faith, not by sight. (2 Corinthians 5:7)

Without faith it is impossible to please him; for he that cometh to God must believe that he is, and that he is a rewarder of them that diligently seek him. (Hebrews 11:6)

Before faith came (before the Word of God came) we were kept under the law, shut up unto the faith which should afterwards be revealed. Wherefore the law was our schoolmaster to bring us unto Christ, that we might be justified by faith. But after that faith is come, we are no longer under a schoolmaster. For, ye are all the children of God, by faith, in Christ Jesus. For as many of you as have been baptized into Christ have put on Christ. There is neither Jew nor Greek, there is neither bond nor free, there is neither male nor female; for ye are all one in Christ Jesus. And if ye be Christ's then are ye Abraham's seed, and heirs according to the promise. (Galatians 3:23–29)

Jesus said, recorded in Matthew 8:11, "Many shall come from the east and west and shall sit down with Abraham and Isaac and Jacob in the kingdom of heaven."

Jesus also said, recorded in Matthew 7:21, "Not everyone that saith unto me, Lord, Lord shall enter into the kingdom of heaven; but he that doeth the will of my Father which is in heaven." This is a hard saying for us today with our man-centered doctrine. But the parable of the ten virgins should tell us who are called to live in these last days, that it would be wise for us to wake up, stir ourselves up, spend time with our King, prepare ourselves for him, surrender to his will, and thereby receive from his hand the oil for our lamps (see Matthew 25:1–13). Isaiah 55:1–3 says, "He that has no money; come, buy and eat… Why do you spend money for that which is not bread and labor for that which satisfies not?

Hearken unto me and eat that which is good and let your soul delight itself...incline your ear and come unto me; hear, and your soul shall live; and I will make an everlasting covenant with you, even the sure mercies of David."

Revelation 3:20 says, "Behold, I stand at the door, and knock; if any man hears my voice, and open the door, I will come into him, and will sup with him, and he with me." Now in the first state, when we open the door and let Jesus in, he will sup with us. This means we are still the lord of the house, and Jesus is the visitor. But as we go on in Christ, the time comes when he is to become Lord of the house, and we are to be supping with him. Oh, how many have been content to have Jesus as a visitor in their house and have never seen fit to make him Lord of the house.

Paul wrote to the Galatians in chapter 4, verse 19, "My little children, of whom I travail in birth again until Christ be formed in you." Oh, how much this is true today, and how we need to travail until Christ be formed in us. We have had a man-centered doctrine and not a God-centered doctrine. We, of understanding, need to travail in birth until we see the kingdom of Christ come. One of my favorite verses is Psalm 53:6 or Psalm 14:7. It is a verse for the intercessor. "Oh! (An intercessor will feel the travail in that "oh!") that the salvation of Israel were come out of Zion! When God brings back the captivity of his people, Jacob shall rejoice, and Israel shall be glad."

Isaiah 26:16–18 says, "Lord, in trouble have they (shall we say "we"?) visited thee, and poured out a prayer when your chastening was upon us. Like as a woman with child, that draws near the time of delivery, is in pain, and cries out in her pangs; so, have we been in your sight, O Lord. We have been with child, we have been in pain, we have as it were brought forth wind; (He said that, not me) we have not wrought any deliverance in the earth; neither have the inhabitants of the world fallen."

Let us pray and intercede that we will all surrender to the King and die to our own desires and allow the King to be the King of our lives.

FLESH VERSUS SPIRIT

Let us consider what Paul said in his letter to the Romans, Romans 9:6–13, "Not as though the word of God hath taken none effect. For they are not all Israel, which are of Israel; neither because they are the seed of Abraham, are they all children; but, *in Isaac shall thy seed be called.* That is, they which are the children born of the flesh, these are not the children of God; but the children of the promise are counted for the seed. For this is the word of promise, *at time will I come and Sarah shall have a son.* And not only this; but Rebecca also had conceived by one, even by our father Isaac; (For the children being not yet born neither having done any good or evil, that the purpose of God according to election might stand, not of works, but of him that called;) it was said unto her, *the elder shall serve the younger.* As it is written, *Jacob have I loved, but Esau have I hated.*" In Genesis 25 we find the story of Isaac and Rebekah in verses 21 through 23: "And Isaac entreated the Lord for his wife, because she was barren: (what a picture of many of our lives today) and the Lord was entreated of him, and Rebekah his wife conceived. And the children struggled together within her; and she said, If it be so, why am I thus? (If this is your promise to me Lord, why is it so hard?) And she went to enquire of the Lord. And the Lord said unto her, two nations are in thy womb and two manners of people shall be separated from thy bowels, and the one people shall be stronger than the other people; and the elder shall serve the younger."

Now let us consider that Esau, the firstborn, is our flesh man, which was born first, and that Jacob is our spirit man, which was born last when we were born again.

> The burden of the Lord to Israel by Malachi. I have loved you saith the Lord. Yet ye say, wherein hast thou loved us? Was not Esau Jacob's brother? saith the Lord; yet I loved Jacob, and I hated Esau and laid his mountains and his heritage waste for the dragons of the wilderness. Whereas Edom saith, we are impoverished, but we will return and build the desolate places; thus, saith the Lord of hosts, they shall build, but I will throw down; and they shall call them, the border of wickedness, and the people against whom the Lord hath indignation forever. And your eyes shall see and ye shall say, the Lord will be magnified from the border of Israel. (Malachi 1:1–5)

And as it is written, "Jacob have I loved, and Esau have I hated." We know that in our flesh dwells no good thing (Romans 7:18). And again, in Isaiah 64:6, it proclaims that all our righteousness is as filthy rags. Romans, chapters 7 and 8 speaks to the struggle that goes on within us.

> For that which I do I allow not; for what I would, that do I not; but what I hate, that do I.

> For I know that in me (that is, in
> my flesh) dwelleth no good thing: for to
> will is present with me; but to perform
> that which is good I find not.
> I find then a law, that, when I
> would do good, evil is present with me.
> (Romans 7:15, 18, 21)

Verse 22 through 25, paraphrased, says, "I delight in the law of God after the spirit man, but I find another law in my flesh man that wars against my spirit man (the law of sin in my flesh). O wretched man that I am! Who shall deliver me from the body of this death? Thank God through Jesus Christ our Lord." Chapter 8, verses 1, 2, and 8 says, "There is therefore now no condemnation to them which are in Christ Jesus, who walk not after the flesh, but after the Spirit. For the law of the Spirit of life in Christ Jesus hath made me free from the law of sin and death. So then they that are in the flesh cannot please God."

Jesus sowed his sinless self that He might bring many sons into glory. And if it be that the Spirit of God dwells in us, then we know that the Spirit, which raised Christ up from the dead, shall also quicken our mortal bodies.

> But as many as received Him, to
> them gave, He power to become the sons
> of God, even to them that believe on his
> name: which were born, not of blood, nor
> of the will of the flesh, nor of the will of
> man, but of God. (John 1:12–13)

> Therefore, we are debtors, not to
> the flesh, to live after the flesh. For if

we live after the flesh, we shall die, but
if we through the Spirit, by the power he
gave us, do mortify the deeds of the body
we shall live. For as many as are led by
the Spirit of God are the sons of God.
(Romans 8: 12–14)

Jesus said in John 10:18, "No man takes my life from
me; I lay it down of myself. I have power to lay it down,
and I have power to take it again." Jesus gave us through the
Holy Spirit the same power to lay down our lives. That is
the power to become the sons of God. Jesus said, "Take up
your cross and follow me." In Philippians 2:5–13, Paul wrote,
paraphrased, "Let the same mind be in you as was in Christ
Jesus; who being God made himself of no reputation, taking
the form of a servant, and was made in the likeness of men
humbled himself and became obedient unto death, even the
death of the cross. Wherefore, my beloved obey working out
your salvation with fear and trembling. It is God working in
you both to will and to do his good pleasure." Man is created
in the image of God, a tri-being: spirit, soul, and body. We
are working out our salvation from the spirit through the
soul and into the body. Just as the children of Israel were to
take the land, so are we to take our souls for the Lord, letting
Him establish the kingdom of God in our lives.

Now, in Genesis 13:17, God told Abram to walk
through the land which he would give to him. And again,
when the children entered the land, in Joshua 1:3, "Every
place that the sole of your foot shall tread upon, that have I
given unto you as I said unto Moses." So we see that the word
or revelation we walk in is the land we receive from God and
that every stronghold that we take, every habit over which we
gain control, every victory, every word that God has spoken

concerning us that we make flesh (the Word becoming flesh in us) shall be our land. God has given us the choice, and it is up to us to walk it out. He did not force Abram, and he will not force us. It is always our choice. He gave us free will.

Now Amalek was the grandson of Esau, born to his son, Eliphaz, through Timna, a concubine, the daughter of Seir (he-goat or devil), a Horite, and he was a prince in Edom. Now the children were at Horeb, where Moses smote the rock, and water came out for the people to drink. The Scripture says, "And they did all drink of that water, which is Christ. The children of Israel had just tempted the Lord, saying, "Is the Lord among us or not? It was at this time the Bible tells us, "Then came Amalek and fought with Israel in Rephidim." Moses told Joshua, "Choose out men, and go fight with Amalek."

> And it came to pass, when Moses
> held up his hand, that Israel prevailed;
> and when he let down his hand, Amalek
> prevailed. (Exodus 17:11)

When we are not spending time with the Lord, and our spirit is weak, that is when Amalek will show up (then came Amalek). And when we press into the Lord and leave up the battle to him, we will prevail.

> And the Lord said unto Moses,
> write this for a memorial in a book, and
> rehearse it in the ears of Joshua; for I
> will utterly put out the remembrance of
> Amalek from under heaven. For he said,
> because the Lord hath sworn that the

Lord will have war with Amalek from
generation to generation. (verses 14, 16)

Notice, while Amalek is to be put out of remembrance,
the battle will be from generation to generation. Your grand-
father fought him. Your dad fought him. You will fight
him. And your children will fight Amalek. Saul was told to
destroy Amalek in 1 Samuel 15, but Saul blew it and lost the
kingdom. David fought Amalek on many occasions, and in
the end, it was an Amalekite that finished off Saul (2 Samuel
1:8–15). Haman was an Amalekite, descendant of Agag, as
well as king Herod of Idumea, who killed all the babies in the
time of Jesus's birth. If you let an Amalekite, go undealt with
in the flesh, you can be sure it will come back to destroy you.

Our flesh, like Esau, will sell our birthright for instant
gratification. It will murmur and take on, as if it was at the
point of death any time it doesn't get its way, just as Esau said,
"I am at the point of death, so what profit is my birthright to
me anyway?" As soon as Esau had eaten and drank, he rose
and went his way, thus he despised his birthright, just as our
flesh will do, unless we, by the Spirit, take it into control.

How do we do this? I am so glad you asked! Let the
spirit in you deal with the flesh the same way we would deal
with an unruly child. You allow the spirit man to discipline
your flesh man, and in the long run, the flesh man will serve
the spirit man. The word of God has declared it! Feed and
speak the word of God to your soul. Fed the proper food; the
soul will serve the spirit. Jesus said in John 6:51, "I am the
living bread which cometh down from heaven; if any man eat
of this bread, he shall live forever; and the bread that I will
give is my flesh; which I will give for the life of the world."
And again, man shall live by every word that proceeds from
the mouth of God. John 1:12 says, "As many as received

Him, to them, He gave power (authority) to become the sons of God." The sons have a birthright. And in verse 13, it says, "Which were born, not of blood, nor of the will of the flesh, nor of the will of man, but of God."

Paul said, "I die daily." It is true? Our flesh will have to die and give in to the spirit daily. We reckon ourselves dead in baptism, but we must walk in the spirit daily. Romans 6:4 says, "Therefore we are buried with him by baptism into death: that like as Christ was raised up from the dead by the glory of the Father, even so we also should walk in newness of life." And again, in Colossians 2:12, Paul wrote, "Buried with him in baptism, wherein also you are risen with him through the faith of the operation of God who raised him from the dead." Remember that Christ gave you the power to become the sons of God (you have the power to lay down your life and power to take it up again) and that without faith in God, it is impossible to please him. Paul wrote in Galatians 2:20, "I am crucified with Christ: nevertheless, I live; yet not I but Christ liveth in me; and the life which I now live in the flesh I live by the faith of the Son of God." In chapter 5, verses 24 through 25, it says, "And they that are Christ's have crucified the flesh with the affection and lusts. If we live in the Spirit, let us also walk in the Spirit."

One of the best ways to crucify the flesh is by fasting. Fasting is not a way for us to show God our dedication to him and guilt him into doing something for us. on the contrary, God has already provided everything for us; it is up to us to move into what God has already provided. The thing that keeps us from doing that is our flesh because it looks at the visible and says what the ten spies said in coming back from spying out the land. It is too hard for us. They are too strong for us. We are like grasshoppers in our own sight, and so we were in their sight. And the flesh will even tell you that it is just being humble, a good cover for all that fear and unbelief (if you buy it). It is all about how you see yourself. Are you looking at the visible, or are you believing what God said? The spirit man, which is the Word of God living in you, says you must speak what God has said. And God has said, "I will bring you in and will destroy your enemies before you." God has said, "I will raise you up by the same Spirit that raised up Christ from the dead," but our fear and unbelief keeps us holding on to the flesh, afraid to die to our flesh and allow God to have his way. The flesh complains, "God brought us out of Egypt to die in the wilderness." As it was then, so is it today, for those things happened to them for examples to us upon who the end of the world should come.

The disciples came to Jesus and said, "We tried to cast out the devil," but we could not.

> And Jesus said unto them, because of your unbelief; for verily I say unto you, if you have faith as a grain of mustard seed, you shall say unto this mountain, remove hence to yonder place; and it shall remove; and nothing shall be impossible unto you. Howbeit, this kind will not go out but by prayer and fasting. (Matthew 17:20–21)

Fasting causes the flesh to become weak, and your spirit man will become stronger. Remember that the devil is a spirit being, and our flesh has no authority over the spirit world. It is only our spirit through the Spirit of Christ's that we have authority over the spirit world and that in the name of Jesus (Yeshua).

I would like to share an experience of mine, which happened over forty years ago when I was fasting. My daughter was under two years old at the time and could just reach the doorknob. My husband had a bad habit of leaving his shaving razor down on the cabinet, just in reach of little hands. I had spoken to him many times about it, but as it was, he just didn't pay attention to such things. One day, I heard the doorknob to the bathroom rattling, so I went to see what it was, and there, covered in blood, was my little girl with the razor in her hand and blood everywhere. You can imagine what went through my mind, from my flesh. This was the first time I ever experienced the division of spirit and flesh so clearly. I believe, because of the fast, the flesh was in slow motion, or at least it seemed to be playing out in slow motion. But it was probably going down so quick that if I had not been fasting at the time, I would have missed it. As I grabbed towels and a washcloth to wipe her down, my flesh came up with all the things which I could scream at my husband, and believe me, they were right and true according to anyone's flesh. But before the flesh could work its deadly work, my spirit spoke and said, "Don't you think he feels bad enough?" I looked at her condition and at him and agreed with my spirit, so I said nothing but continued to wipe away the blood and was prepared to put on a lot of Band-Aids. But do you know, as I wiped away the blood, there was not one cut or one place for a Band-Aid. That is when God started to show me the division between the spirit man and the flash. And I can't say that I've always walked in the spirit, but I will never forget that experience, and I know that fasting will weaken the loud voice of your flesh and that if you will start fasting, you will really begin hearing the still, small voice of your spirit and that God has already given you the power to obey that voice. All you must do is agree with him. I personally believe, our flesh never gets any better. We are just to make the choice to live in the spirit instead of the flesh.

Let me illustrate it another way. Pretend you are a computer, and when you got born again by the Spirit, that was a new upgraded software. You turn on the computer, and up comes the new program. It is so nice. You love the feeling, and it can do all kinds of great things. Someone might ask you if you have that new software on your computer. "O, yes," you say, "it is so nice now. My computer can go to heaven." Then they ask, "How does it work?" You explain, "I haven't used it yet. The old program is so easy and comfortable for me. I just haven't made the switch," or "I only use it sometimes. The old one is so comfortable and easy to use." This is where many Christians are today. They have the Spirit loaded on their computer, but they seldom use the Spirit. the old flesh is so comfortable and easy to use. So what fasting will do is slow down your computer and bring both applications up at the same time. So you can decide each time which applications to use until you become comfortable, and the use of the new God-given spirit program becomes natural.

Some will ask, "What type of fast to go on, and how long should I fast?" First, if your health or job is such that you must eat, then go on a partial fast, as Daniel did. I don't want to pretend to tell anyone else what they should do, and this is not medical advice. Always consult a doctor if you have a medical condition. But I will make some suggestions, like drinking juices and eating only foods that you don't like but are good for you, such as fresh fruits and vegetables; baked potatoes without anything on them; no pastes, bread, or pleasant foods; nothing pleasant to your flesh. You can purchase pulse on the web by looking up Daniel's food and the word pulse. It is dried fruits and vegetables and grains, dried and ground to a pulse; this was the trail mix of Daniel's day. When the people of that time were on long travels, they would carry it in a pouch and snack on it as needed (it is not inexpensive; however, it is good), otherwise not eating at all and only drinking water or water and juice. Psalm 131:2 says "Surely, I have behaved and quieted myself, as a child that is weaned of his mother; my soul is even as a weaned child." The Amplified says (ceased from fretting), this is the key to how long to fast. The first fast should be as long as it takes for your flesh to stop fretting. The next fast will go until the flesh stops fretting, plus some time; the next until flesh stops fretting, plus a little longer; etc. The time it will take for the flesh to stop fretting will get shorter each time, and the Spirit will get stronger each time. You will begin to see and recognize the difference between the flesh and the Spirit. And by fretting, I mean it may throw a real fit, as Esau. It will claim to be dying. Tell it that is fine; that is what you are supposed to do.

I will just paraphrase Isaiah 22:9–14 here: God said he saw the breaches (weakness) of the house of David and how they sought for the waters of the old pool (the old moves of God) but did not look to the Maker thereof, nor showed respect to him that fashioned it long ago. For in that day, the Lord called for weeping, mourning, baldness, and girding of sackcloth (the way people repented in those days). But I get joy and gladness, slaying oxen, killing sheep, eating and drinking, and saying tomorrow (manana) we will die. It was revealed in my ears by the Lord of host. Surely this iniquity shall not be purged from us till we die.

Many Christians don't hear form God because they don't recognize his voice. And of course, this opens us up to deception. Many people don't know the difference between their spirit, their soul, and any other visitors that may be hanging out there; they just think it is all of them and that,

that is just the way I am. If we are going to see changes, we need to make some changes.

For every trial we go through, there is a death. We die to pride, selfishness, opinions, religious beliefs, etc. We die to ourselves, and there is a resurrection, a new you. This is how we all go from glory to glory.

> Fret not because of evildoers neither be envious against workers of iniquity; trust in the Lord, and do good, so shall you dwell in the land; delight yourself in the Lord, and He will give you the desires of your heart; commit your way unto the Lord, and he will bring it to pass; and He will bring forth your righteousness as the light, and your judgment as the noonday. Rest in the Lord, wait patiently, fret not, cease from anger, give up wrath, fret not yourself in any way to do evil. (Psalm 37:1–8)

Verse 9 says, "For evildoers shall be cut off; but those that wait upon the Lord, they shall inherit the earth." And he will give you the desires of your heart, which means he will change your desires, give you his desires, his desires becoming our desires.

We are told, the prophet Samuel was brought unto the house of God when his mother, Hannah, had weaned him at that time. She presented him to God and left him with Eli, the priest. Frankly, I always thought I'd need a lot of faith to leave any child with Eli, who had not done such a good job with his own sons. But Hannah was not leaving her son with Eli; she was leaving Samuel with God. What faith she had.

And when we look at the story, we are awed by the way God used Samuel. We are told that the word of the Lord was rare at that time. And from the picture we get of that time, it is easy to understand why the word of the Lord was rare. Now, in 1 Samuel 3:7, it says, "Now Samuel did not yet know the Lord, neither was the Word of the Lord yet revealed unto him." So we see that the revelation of the Word of the Lord is key to knowing the Lord. But in verse 19, it says, "And Samuel grew, and the Lord was with him, and did let none of his words fall to the ground." Verse 21 says, "And the Lord appeared again, in Shiloh; for the Lord revealed himself to Samuel, in Shiloh, by the Word of the Lord." It is the Word of God. And knowing him, that brings revelation.

It is his Word, that works in us both to know and to do his will. Without that Word working, God simply cannot trust us. I want to go into another of the Bible stories to explain my point. God's book tells it all—the good, the bad, and the ugly.

Now Elisha had picked up the mantle of Elijah. And he took the mantle of Elijah and smote the waters and said, "Where is the Lord God of Elijah?" And the waters parted, and Elisha went over (2 Kings 2:14). And Elisha went up from Bethel. And as he was going up by the way, there came forth little children out of the city and mocked him and said unto him, "Go up, thou bald head. Go up, thou bald head." And Elisha turned back and looked on them and cursed them in the name of the Lord. (Remember, it is with our words that we rule.) And there came forth two she bears out of the wood, and tare forty-two children of them (verse 22–24). To me, this is one of the hardest parts of the Bible to read. But you know that the Bible tells it the way it is— the good, the bad, and the ugly. Remember that Elisha had wanted a double portion of what Elijah had, and many today

also think that is what they want, a double portion of someone else's ministry. Many a sermon has been preached about
the double portion without consideration of the awesome
responsibility that goes with it. Elisha had not walked it out
in God as Elijah had. Elijah's power came from a relationship
with God. But Elisha's came from a relationship with Elijah
in the beginning, and he had to move on to a relationship
with God, which gave him control to his power. We know
this was in the early part of Elisha's ministry, with a mantle
he got from Elijah, and it is possible that Elisha had not yet
realized the power that was in his words, much like many of
God's children of today, which speak all kinds of death and
negative words over themselves and others. Can you image
what would happen in just twenty-four hours if God gave his
church a small portion of the power they are asking him to
give them? Let's face it, we must truly make him King of our
lives before he can trust us with his power. The real question
is, can God trust us, not can we trust God?

Daniel 11:32–33, speaking of the last days, says, "And
such as do wickedly against the covenant shall he, corrupt
by flatteries; but the people that do know their God shall be
strong, and do exploits. And they that understand among
the people shall instruct many." So it is the people that know
their God that shall do exploits. Revelation 17:14 says, "He is
Lord of lords and King of kings, and they that are with him
are called, chosen and faithful."

KNOWING GOD

Did you ever read a verse in the Bible and just think, *I will never be able to do that*? I am sure that we all have experienced this at some time or the other. For me, one of those verses was 2 Corinthians 5:16, which says, "Wherefore henceforth know we no man after the flesh; yea, though we have known Christ after the flesh, yet now henceforth know we him no more." Let's go on and read verse 17: "Therefore, if any man be in Christ, he is a new creature; old things are passed away; behold, all things are become new."

It was the "know no man after the flesh" part that was getting me. I told God I just can't do that; I don't know how. I would read the verse and see if there was anyone I could know after the spirit, and, no, not even one person came to mind. I read the verse over and over. Finally he told me to put the word *person* in the place of the word *man*, and I kept reading. I was going to read the verse until it became clear. Finally, the Lord said unto me, "Are you a person?" I said yes, and then the answer became clear. In order to know another person after the Spirit, I must get to know my own spirit man first. Spirit knows spirit, and flesh knows flesh! We did know Christ after the flesh, as recorded in the scriptures. But now, Paul said, "Know him that way no more." Now *know Christ after the Spirit*. Get to know the new spirit man of your own heart, then everyone else begins to look better. Getting to know your own spirit man takes time spent in the presence of the Lord. Some of us, it would seem, want to do all the talking when we are in the presence of the Lord, bringing our list, complaints, and troubles unto him, and then we are off to our busy lives. Do you know of any other king that you would treat that way? Probably not. He is the Creator of the world, universe, and all things; in time and outside time. He sees our life from beginning to end in one glance, having all knowledge, and he loves you and wants to share his knowledge with you. It is at these times that maybe we should feel a little ashamed for wanting to eat from the tree of knowledge instead of finding out from the Spirit, his will, and obeying him. He is a God that wants communion with his children, and we don't have time for him. He died for us. His wife and we do not have time to spend with him. Can't you just feel his broken heart?

Listen to Ephesians 5:25–32.

> Husbands, love your wives, even as Christ also loved the church, and gave himself for it; that he might sanctify and cleanse it with the washing of water by the word (rhema). That he might present it to himself a glorious church, not having spot, or wrinkle, or any such thing; but that it should be holy and without blemish. So, ought men to love their wives as their own bodies. He that loves his wife loves himself. For no man ever yet hated his own flesh; but nourishes and cherishes it even as the Lord the church; for we are members of his body, of his flesh, and of his bones. For this cause shall a man leave his father and mother, and shall be

> joined unto his wife, and they two shall
> be one flesh. This is a great mystery; but I
> speak concerning Christ and the Church.

Ephesians 1:9–11, paraphrased, says, "Having made known unto us the mystery of his will, according to his good pleasure, which he hath proposed in himself, that in the fullness of time, he might gather into one all things in Christ, all things in heaven and in earth, even in him." Do you realize that the angels desire to investigate the plans that Christ has for us and that making us one with himself, he has raised us up above all his other creations, angels, principalities, and rulers in high places? Yes, even if you are the smallest cell on his little toe, you are above principalities, powers, and dominions. Ephesians 3:10 says, "To the intent that now unto the principalities and powers in heavenly places might be known *by the church* the manifold wisdom of God."

> What is man, that thou art mind-
> ful of him? And the son of man, that
> thou visitest him? For thou hast made
> him a little lower than the angels, and
> hast crowned him with glory and honor.
> Thou madest him to have dominion over
> the works of thy hands; thou hast put all
> things under his feet. (Psalm 8:4–6)

Abram was called a friend of God, and he said, "Will I keep from him the thing that I am going to do?" God is looking for friends today to share his plans with. He told the disciples, when the Spirit of truth comes, he will guide you into all truth; for he shall not speak of himself. He shall take of mine and shall show it unto you, and he shall show you things to come (taken from John 16:7–15).

> Henceforth I call you not servants,
> for the servant knows not what the lord
> doeth; but I have called you friends; for
> all things that I have heard of my Father I
> have made known unto you. (John 15:15)

Listen to Paul's prayer of the Ephesians in Ephesians 3:16–19, paraphrased: "That they would be strengthened with might by his Spirit in the inner man, that Christ may dwell in your hearts by faith, that you would be rooted and grounded in love, that you would be able to comprehend with all saints what is the breadth and length and depth and height; and to know the love of Christ, which passes knowledge, that you might be filled with all the fullness of God."

> Howbeit when he the Spirit of
> Truth, is come he will guide you into all
> truth; for he shall not speak of himself,
> but whatsoever he shall hear that shall
> he speak, and he will show you things
> to come. He shall glorify me for he shall
> receive of mine and shall show it unto
> you. All things that the father hath are
> mine, therefore said I that he shall take
> of mine and show it unto you. (John
> 16:13–15)

> The Holy Spirit shall teach you
> in the same hour what ye ought to say.
> (Luke 12:12)

58

In Hebrews 8:6, God, through Jesus, mediated a better covenant established upon better promises for us.

> For the law makes men high priests which have infirmity; but the word of the oath, which was since the law, makes the son, who is consecrated for evermore. (Hebrews 7:28)

God is looking for relationship with his creation. So God made a new covenant with them and set out to keep both side of the covenant. He said, "The day will come when I will sprinkle clean water upon you and cleanse you. A new heart will I give you, and a new spirit will I put within you. And I will take away the stony heart out of your flesh, and I will give you a heart of flesh. I will put *my Spirit within you and cause you to walk* in my statutes, and you will keep my judgments and do them, hearing and responding to God! After that, I will multiply the fruit of the tree and the increase of the field, and you will receive no more reproach. I, the Lord, have spoken it, and I will do it." Thus, says the Lord God, "I will yet for this be enquired of by the house of Israel to do it for them" (from Ezekiel 36). Notice that God wants us to ask him to do it, even though he could just do it, which is what I think many Christians think that if God wants it, he will do it. No, he has chosen to partner with his children.

In Genesis 22, we see the nature of God in not withholding his only begotten and beloved Son. We see the faith of Abraham in obedience to God and in his words as he told Isaac, "God will provide himself a lamb for a burnt offering." The part we hear so little about is Isaac's part. Now Abraham was over a hundred years old, and Isaac was a strong young man, probably in his twenties, and could have easily out run his father. I don't know about you, but if that was me, my flesh man, I would be the sacrifice when you catch me, old man. (This is our flesh seeking to save itself, and it is the natural fleshly way.) Yet Isaac surrendered to the point of letting his father bind him and place him on the altar upon the wood. In Genesis 22:2, God said to Abraham, take your only (*yachid*—meaning sole, solitary) son. But when he came to verse 12, it says, "I know that thou fearest God, seeing thou hast not withheld thy son, thine only son from me." God changed the word only to (*yahad*—meaning united together, become one, join, or unite) son. This same word is translated unite in other places, to become one. The son of God was united with Isaac (the son of the promise) in the willingness to offer himself as the sacrifice. And as we (*yahad*) become one with Him, we are also united with Isaac in the willingness to be offered. We too were in the loins of Isaac upon the rock when we, *yahad*, become one with his Son (see John 17) and enter his death, for he died as us, taking upon himself our sin nature, that we might live as him, taking upon us his righteous nature. To "as many as received him, to them gave he power (authority) to become the sons of God, even to them that believe on his name. Which were born not of blood, nor of the will of the flesh, nor of the will of man, but of God" (John 1:12–13).

The Word tells us to present ourselves to the Lord as a living sacrifice. So many of us present ourselves and then keep getting up off the altar. Is there anyone that doesn't relate to this? We know that even Jesus sweat blood in the garden when he set his will with the Father's will. I am going to share a scripture for this, which the Lord shared with me, which I believe will be helpful to you as well. You might be familiar with Matthew 18:18: "Whatsoever you shall bind on earth shall be bound in heaven and whatsoever you loose on earth shall be loosed in heaven." But you might not be as familiar with Psalm 118:27 in this context: "God is the Lord, which hath showed us light; bind the sacrifice with cords, even unto the horns of the altar." So you can see that the first thing that should ever be bound is ourselves as the sacrifice to the horns of the altar. This is done daily, and it is a choice of our will as we use our words to speak the surrender of our wills to his will.

Jesus said, "Whosoever seeks to save his life shall lose it, and whosoever shall lose his life for my sake shall find it." We find a new life in him. Let us rise to the battle, take the land, and establish the kingdom unto the King of kings. This requires a growth process. John wrote in 1 John 2:12,

> I write unto you, little children because your sins are forgiven you for his name's sake (the blood of the Lamb). I write unto young men because the word of God abides in you, you are strong and have overcome the wicked one (by the word of their testimony). I write to you, fathers, because you have known him that is from the beginning. (They loved not their lives unto the death, knowing the nature of God.) (1 John 2:12–14)

> They overcame him by the blood of the Lamb, and by the word of their testimony, and they loved not their lives unto the death. (Revelation 12:11)

> I have written unto you, fathers, because ye have known him that is from

the beginning, I have written unto you,
young men, because ye are strong, and
the word of God abides in you, and ye
have overcome the wicked one. (1 John
2:14)

It is through the Word of God dwelling in us that we
will overcome the wiles of the dark forces.

In 1 Chronicles 12:32, we are told of the children of
Issachar, who understood the times and knew what Israel
ought to do. In their time, as it is in our time, it was the time
to establish the throne to the true King. As it is today, there
was a parallel kingdom, the kingdom of Saul and the kingdom of David. Today it is the kingdom of Lucifer and his
dark forces and the kingdom of God and his elect lady called
out ones. Those of understanding of the times will know,
as the children of Issachar, that we are to come to the battle
and battle to establish the kingdom to the true King. All of
David's mighty men came for the purpose of establishing the
kingdom to the true king.

A word more on the parallel kingdoms, both King
David and King Saul were anointed by Samuel. In 1 Samuel
24, Saul entered a cave that David and his men were hiding
in, and his men said, "The Lord hath delivered Saul into your
hand." But David just cut off Saul's skirt and said, "The Lord
forbid that I should do this thing unto my master, the Lord's
anointed, to stretch forth mine hand against him. Seeing he
is the anointed of the Lord." And David called unto Saul to
show him the piece of the garment and said, "Mine hand
spared thee, and I said I will not put forth mine hand against
my lord, for he is the Lord's anointed. Moreover, my father,
see yea, see the skirt of thy robe in my hand, for in that I
cut off the skirt of thy robe and killed thee not. Know thou

and see that there is neither evil nor transgression in mine hand, and I have not sinned against thee. Yet thou huntest my soul to take it. The Lord judge between me and thee, and the Lord avenge me of thee. But mine hand shall not be upon thee." And again, in 1 Samuel 26:9–11, it says, "And David said to Abishai, destroy him not, for who can stretch forth his hand against the Lord's anointed and be guiltless? David said furthermore; as the Lord liveth, the Lord shall smite him, or his day shall come to die, or he shall descend into battle and perish. The Lord forbid that I should stretch forth mine hand against the Lord's anointed."

In another place, Jude 9 tells us that Michael the archangel, when contending with the devil, disputed about the body of Moses, did not bring against him a railing accusation but said, "The Lord rebuke thee." Man rushes in where angels fear to tread.

As I write this book, I know that I am sacrificing many holy cows, and I want any defender of holy cows to know that there will be no hard feelings, and they are already forgiven.

ENTERING THE
KINGDOM

Jesus said in Matthew 18:3–4, "Except you be converted, and become as little children, you shall not enter into the kingdom of heaven. Whosoever shall humble himself as this little child, the same is greatest in the kingdom of heaven." Notice the word *converted*. Man was created with the spirit on the outside, communing with God. But when sin came, that spirit went on the inside of man and began the dying process. That spirit was the light covering that Adam and Eve had, so they did not know that they were naked. Now, in the kingdom of God, man must be converted and once again live from the spirit made alive toward God by his Spirit, not our souls, and in communion with God once again. Our bodies will stay the same until this corruptible put on the incorruptible at the second coming of Christ. In 1 Corinthians 15:44–45, it says, "It is sown a natural body; it is raised a spiritual body... The first man Adam was made a living soul; the last Adam was made a quickening spirit." Death will be the last enemy to be put underfoot (1 Corinthians 15:26).

We must humble ourselves (soul nature) as a little child who has not yet become so self-conscious as to condemn or justify himself and thereby not be able to receive from God the free gift. Paul wrote in 2 Corinthians 10:12 to not measure themselves by themselves and compare themselves among themselves. This is why Jesus said in Matthew 5:3–5, "Blessed are the poor in spirit; for theirs is the kingdom of heaven. Blessed are they that mourn; for they shall be comforted. Blessed are the meek; for they shall inherit the earth." We could say today, "Blessed are they that understand the poorness of their own condition and are meek enough to receive from God. They will enter the kingdom."

In the Old Testament days, God's kingdom was limited to the chosen descendants of Abraham. Satan is, as the Bible calls, subtle (capable of making or noticing fine distinctions in meaning, mental keenness, delicately skillful or clever, delicately suggestive, not grossly obvious, working insidiously, not easily detected). I put this meaning in because he still works in the same way, and we should be on the lookout for his ways. He was successful in getting his authority back from man. Man had lost the position God had given him, and now he must also lose the right to the tree of life, lest he eat and live forever in his sinful state. Jesus is the tree of life, the Word of God is life.

> So he drove out the man; and he
> placed at the east of the garden of Eden
> a cherub, and a flaming sword which
> turned every way, to keep the way of the
> tree of life. (Genesis 3:24)

From that time until Jesus came the first time, God's dealing with man was through a veil of angelic authority. This is why we see God as a vengeful God in the Old Testament and a God of mercy in the New Testament. God did not change. It is just that man did not have a revelation of God, except for the prophets of old, like Moses, Samuel, Elijah, David, and others, which God used to communicate.

What we see was God as revealed through the veil of angels, which were keeping man from God. These angels were working for the kingdom of darkness. He is still the angel of the Lord. And in many places, we see him so called, even as the death angel that went forth in Egypt and the angel king David dealt with in 2 Samuel 24:1 and 1 Chronicles 21:1 and in Zechariah 3:6. The angel of the Lord did protest when Joshua was receiving his garments and crown. He brought forth the law book and quoted, "If thou wilt walk in my ways and if thou wilt keep my charges." In my imagination, I had a few years of law. I hear him say, "If it pleases the court, your honor, allow me to present exhibit A." Then he brings forth a large blown-up picture of the filthy garments. These were our filthy garments, and I believe that was the last time Lucifer was allowed to be in the courts of heaven. It was finished. The innocent blood had been poured out on the altar in heaven, and Lucifer was banned from the council of the holy ones.

Jesus is the revelation of God. He said, "If you have seen me, you have seen the Father. And it is his plan to unfold his revelation through himself and his body and to make known to man, as well as principalities and powers, the true nature of God."

In Ephesians 3:9–10, Paul said his ministry was "to make all men see what is the fellowship of the mystery which from the beginning of the world, has been hid in God who created all things by Jesus Christ. To the intent that now unto the principalities and powers in heavenly places might be known *by the church* the manifold wisdom of God."

Just as man is three parts, so was the tabernacle in the wilderness, and so is the heavenly tabernacle. The veil in the tabernacle was to be covered with cherubim and was placed between the holy place and the most holy place (Exodus

26:31). Remember, when Jesus died on the cross, the veil of the temple was rent in twain from the top to the bottom, as was the veil (angelic rule) in the heavens (Matthew 27:51). Jesus came, lived, and died to undo what had been done by the first Adam in the garden and to restore the communication between man and God.

Jesus said in John 6:63, "It is the Spirit that quickeneth; the flesh profiteth nothing; the words that I speak unto you, they are Spirit, and they are Life."

> In the beginning was the Word, and the Word was with God, and the Word was God. The same was in the beginning with God. All things were made by him and without him was not anything made that was made. In him was life, and the life was the light of men. And the light shineth in darkness and the darkness comprehended it not. (John 1:1–5)

Jesus, the Word of God, God speaks his Word, and where the Word goes, so does the breath of God by whom the world was created, came to earth in the flesh of man to reveal to us the true nature of God, which is love. He died as us and poured out his blood to deliver us from the power of darkness and has translated us into his kingdom.

> Who is the image of the invisible God the firstborn of very creature. For by him were all things created, that are in heaven and that are in earth, *visible and invisible*, whether they be thrones or dominions, or principalities, or pow-

ers; all things were created by him and
for him. He is the head of the body, the
church; who, is the beginning, the firstborn from the dead; that in all things he
might have the preeminence. (Colossians
1:15–16, 18)

As Jesus imaged the Father, so ought man to image
Jesus. Jesus, having taken upon himself the flesh, will forever
have a body like ours.

Unto every one of us is given grace
according to the measure of the gift of
Christ. Wherefore he said, when He
ascended on high, He led captivity cap-
tive, and gave gifts unto men. Now that
He ascended, what is it but that he also
descended first into the lower parts of
the earth? He that descended is the same
also that ascended for above all heavens,
that He might fill all things. (Ephesians
4:7–10)

Disarming principalities and powers, he made a show
out of them openly, triumphing over them (Colossians 2:15).
And he took back the authority from Satan (rent the veil) and
took his sinless blood and ascended unto the Father (see John
20:17) and, once and for all, paid the price for sin, restoring
relationship with man. The only question now is, what will
you and I do with this information? Will we receive his gift
and move into his kingdom and give him his rightful position as our King?

There was a man of the tribe of Benjamin who lived in the days of Saul. His name was Rechab, and he told his sons not to drink wine and not to plant vineyards or sow seeds and not to build house but to live in tents. Now, in the days of Jeremiah, these sons were still living their lives in obedience to their father, Rechab. The word of the Lord came to Jeremiah, saying, "Go get the Rechabites and set wine before them and say unto them, 'Drink.'" But the sons said, "We will not drink wine because our father, Jonadab, the son of Rechab, commanded us, saying, 'You shall drink no wine, neither you nor your sons, forever. In Jeremiah 35, it says that then the word of the Lord came to Jeremiah, saying, "Thus says the Lord of hosts, the God of Israel, 'Go say to the men of Judah.'"

"Will you not receive instruction to hearken to my words?" said the Lord. "The words of Jonadab, the son of Rechab, that he commanded his sons not to drink wine are kept until this day. And I rising early and speak to you, and you will not hearken unto me."

This is the heart of God. He wants his children to receive from him; and he was hurt that Rechab's sons would obey their earthly father's voice, but his children would not obey him. You know, as a parent, I can really relate to God in this matter.

Obedience to God is the first step to entering his kingdom.

> We have had fathers of our flesh which corrected us, and we gave them reverence; shall we not much rather be in subjection unto the Father of spirits, and live? (Hebrews 12:9)

> And I will put enmity between thee (Satan) and the woman, and between thy seed and her seed. And Adam called his wife's name Eve; because she was the mother of all living. (Genesis 3:15, 20)

Just as Eve, the wife of the first Adam, is the mother of all living after the flesh, so the church, the wife of Jesus, is the mother of all spiritual life in the earth realm. The soul of man is the only thing that bridges between the spirit world and the visible world; and it is the womb of God. God has chosen to work through his church; this is why we are to be faithful and to know him. out of this relationship comes the life of the spirit. Because of the enmity between the woman and Satan, we find a barren womb a problem among the seed of the promise. Sarah, Rebecca, Rachel, Hanna, and Elizabeth all had this problem. While those of the world were living in (fleshly) blessings, the women of faith needed to seek God to open their womb (soul) to receive blessings. So it is with the church we must always be seeking God to be fruitful. Jesus said in Matthew 7:17–20 (among other places), "A good tree brings forth good fruit; but a corrupt tree brings forth evil fruit. A good tree cannot bring forth evil fruit neither can a corrupt tree bring forth good fruit. Every tree that brings not forth good fruit is hewn down and cast into the fire."

We only bring forth good fruit from our time spent with him (relationship). If we do not come and seek him (abide in him) on our own, he will allow circumstances to drive us to seek him; this is because he loves us so much. So seeking God is necessary for entering the kingdom. Read the prophet Hosea, whose wife brought forth life from another source, and you will understand God's grief when we bear fruit but not by him. He calls this spiritual adultery.

The soul of man is more precious than silver and gold because it is the only thing that bridges the gulf between the spirit world and the natural world. This is why wars are being fought over the soul of man. The soul is the womb of God. God needs it in order to produce his fruit into the earth rim, and also Satan wants to use it to prove his point, produce his seed, and overcome God. So you see, God does have an enemy, and that same enemy is your enemy. This is why God says, "Count my enemy as your enemy, as I count your enemies as my enemies." Revelation 18:13 states that Babylon deals in the soul of men, among all the other things. Verse 20, paraphrased, says, "Rejoice over her fall, thou heavens and apostles and prophets. God has avenged you on her."

We are told in Philippians 4:6, "Be careful for nothing; but in everything by prayer and supplication with thanksgiving let your request be made known unto God." Jesus said in John 16:23b–24 "Whatsoever you shall ask the Father in my name, he will give it you. Hitherto have you asked nothing in my name; ask, and you shall receive, that your joy may be full." In Ephesians 3:19–20, Paul prays for us to know the love of Christ, which passes knowledge, that we would be filled with all the fullness of God. Now, unto him that is able, to do exceedingly abundantly above all that we ask or think, according to the power that works in us. If we are allowing God's Spirit to work in us, there will be no good thing withheld from us, and we will have our petition.

> And this is the confidence that we have in him, that, if we ask anything according to his will, he heareth us; and if we know that he hears us, whatsoever we ask, we know that we have the petitions that we desired of him. (1 John 5:14–15)

And in Psalm 37:4, it says, "Delight yourself in the Lord, and He will give you the desires of your heart." Your desires will be his desires because he has given them to you! Oh, how many prayer meetings are held without ever finding out from God what is on his heart for a prayer concern. What does he want you to do in the heavens today?

God's desire is a people that will come to him and pray heaven's will to earth instead of earth's will to heaven. Then we will enter true spiritual warfare, directed by the captain of the host, as well as the captain of our souls.

The Lord has declared our enemies as his enemies, and we are to declare his enemies as our enemies and to put his enemies under his feet. Ephesians 6:12–17 says that we wrestle not against flesh and blood but against principalities, powers, against the rulers of darkness of this world, against spiritual wickedness in high places. So take the whole armor of God that you may be able to stand in the evil day. Stand therefore, having your loins girt about with truth and having on the breastplate of righteousness; and your feet shod with the good news of peace. Above all take the shield of faith that you shall be able to quench all the fiery darts of the wicked. And take the helmet of salvation and the sword of the Spirit, which is the word of God. The Lord has given us his Word that we will be able to war a good warfare. His Word will not return to him void, but it will accomplish that which he pleases. "And it shall prosper in the thing whereto I sent it," says the Lord. If we declare his Word, we will see the power of his kingdom. He said, "Let God's word be true and every man a liar." Our experiences are just that, our experience, but God's word is the truth, no matter our experience. And when we put our experiences above God's word, we are calling God a liar. The children of Israel failed to enter in because of their words. And the Lord said, "As you have spoken in my ear, so

will I do it to you. I will surely do it unto this evil congregation that are gathered together against me" (Numbers 14:28,
35). When they spoke from their feeling instead of his Word,
he called that evil, which is *live* backward.

> For Jerusalem is ruined and Judah
> is fallen; because their tongue and their
> doings are against the Lord. (Isaiah 3:8)

Our choice is to declare the Word of God the Creator of
the heaven and earth, who is outside of time and space and
knows our life from beginning to end in one glance, or we
can trust our souls, intellect, and emotions and declare what
seems right to us. I am told that a pilot, when flying by controls, has to learn to follow the controls, no matter what their
senses are telling them, because to trust their own senses is
to fly the airplane into the ground. That is very much what
many well-meaning people are doing today by putting our
trust into the things that are visible instead of the invisible
Word of God. Remember, the things that are visible were
created from the things that are invisible.

Remember Amalek, the prince in Edom we dis-
cussed earlier? Deuteronomy 25:17–19, paraphrased, says,
"Remember what Amalek did unto you by the way, when ye
were come forth out of Egypt, how he met you by the way
and smote you in the back when you were faint and weary
and feared not God." Notice how the enemy came when the
children were faint and weary and hit them in the back; this
is still his tactic. Believe me, he is no gentleman. Therefore, it
shall be, when the Lord your God has given you rest from all
your enemies, roundabout in the land which the Lord, your
God, gives you to possess for an inheritance. You shall blot
out the remembrance of Amalek from under the heavens. You

must not forget it. There are spiritual and fleshly enemies we fight in our land, enemies which will have to be taken out of remembrance by the power of the Holy Spirit. If these Amalekites are not destroyed and put out of remembrance, they will cause us to miss the mark and fly our planes into the ground. If we trust their own emotions and not God's word, we will make shipwreck our lives. And of course this makes life a lot harder than it needs to be.

Jesus, speaking with the disciples just before the crucifixion, said, "The prince of this world cometh, and hath nothing in me" (John 14:30b). If Satan can find anything of his in us, he can control us. But of course, because nothing of his was in Jesus, he could not control Jesus. Therefore, he could not take Jesus's life; Jesus laid it down of himself. Here I want to share a revelation which the Lord shared with me. You have heard this earthly truth: To every action, there is an equal reaction. You know, currently, that there are two kingdoms in operation here on earth and that they have very different ways of operating. The earthly way is to get all you can. God's way is to give. In the earthly kingdom they that are great, lord it over you. In God's kingdom, those that would be great are the servants of all. In God's kingdom, nothing is to be done in a reaction; the Spirit only acts. Reaction comes from the soul based on the five senses and is earthly. The acts of the Spirit come from obedience to the Spirit of God. Jesus said, "I can do nothing of myself. I only do and say those things which the Father says and does." Remember when Jesus cleansed the temple? If that had been done in reaction, it would have been sin. But because it was in obedience to the Father, it was an act of the Spirit. Hence, we have a whole book in the Bible called the Acts of the Apostles.

Now here is the revelation: Because of reaction, Satan's kingdom works like this. We all are like balls on a billiard table. He can hit one ball in a certain way and just stand back and call the other balls as he pockets us. He is an expert on human behavior. This works only if we are operating from reaction, in our flesh and soul realm, his kingdom. The enemy uses the five senses to enter our souls. This is why we must, through the Spirit, mortify the deeds of the flesh and begin to operate with the spirit in control of our souls and bodies.

Our intellect and emotions make great servants for the spirit, but they make very bad masters. In Bible times, when Israel was obedient to God, we are told that Edom paid tribute. But when it is recorded that Israel walked not according to God, Edom appointed a king over themselves and often came against Israel in war. So it is today. If we are not walking in the spirit of God, we find the flesh man (Edom) battling us. Everything in this world encourages us to live by our emotions. Just follow your heart, they will say. May our answer be, "No, I will follow the spirit."

> Blow the trumpet in Zion, and sound an alarm in my holy mountain let all the inhabitants of the land tremble; for the day of the Lord cometh, for it is nigh at hand; a day of darkness and of gloominess, a day of clouds and of thick darkness. And the Lord shall utter his voice before his army; for his camp is very great; for He is strong that executes his word; for the day of the Lord is great and very terrible; and who can abide it? (Joel 2:1–2a, 11)

The answer is them that execute his word. That day is upon us. Now is the time. Who is it that has his light in these dark times? When there is a light in your clay vessel, as with Gideon's army, when the trumpet sounded, every vessel was broken, and they shouted the sword of the Lord and stood every man in his place. Then confusion and fear came upon the enemy, and they turned their swords against their fellows. Praise to God who is mighty in battle.

When the enemy's devices return upon him, oh, what joy and gladness in the day of Purim. Esther was a godly queen in the kingdom of Media Persia, and Haman (vizier, an underruler in the Babylon Kingdom in the Ottoman Empire, and it is the name Hitler used for his underrulers) was the enemy of God's people. God brought her to the kingdom for such a time as this. And when she went to the king, this is what he said, "I have given you the house of your enemy and the king's ring. Write a new decree. Write according to your will, and seal it with the king's seal." This is the decree that went forth in that day, that Israel should stand against the decree to destroy and to slay, to arm themselves and to fight for their lives, to fight for their brothers, their children, and their wives.

"My queen, they have slain five hundred in Shushan alone, not to mention throughout all my throne. What could I do more for you?"

"My king, if I have found favor in your sight grant to my people to have another day such as this."

And it was granted. You can only hang Haman and his ten sons once. I believe, the second day is a prophetic day that we might destroy the Antichrist and his ten horns. When the enemy's devices return upon him, oh, what joy and gladness in the day of Purim.

THE DAY OF THE LORD

We know that from Malachi 4:5–6, it says, "I will send you Elijah the prophet before the coming of the great and dreadful day of the Lord. And he shall turn the heart of the fathers to the children, and the heart of the children to their fathers, lest I come and smite the earth with a curse." In Matthew 11:13–15 Jesus said, "For all the prophets and the law prophesied until John. And if ye will receive it, this is Elias which was for to come. He that hath ears to hear let him hear." And in Matthew 17:10–13, Jesus spoke again. "And his disciples asked him, saying, why then say the scribes that Elias must first come?" And Jesus answered and said unto them, "Elias truly shall first come and restore all things." But I say unto you that Elias has come already, and they knew him not but have done unto him whatsoever they listed. Likewise shall also the Son of Man suffer of them. Then the disciples understood that he spoke unto them of John the Baptist. It is obvious that Jesus called John the Baptist the Spirit of Elias and said the people of his generation did not recognize him.

Now there may be a real Elijah coming for the real Jewish people in the last days; I am not addressing that in this book but rather the spirit of Elias that was sent to prepare the way of the Lord, the spirit that came before his first coming to earth. Malachi tells us, "I will send you, Elijah the prophet, before the coming of the great and dreadful day of the Lord." I believe that same spirit is coming to hail his second coming, and that spirit is calling the spirit of the children of God to the Father. A people that will make King Jesus the King in their lives and fulfill God's will on earth will again usher in his kingdom.

And Jesus said in Luke 7:28, "For I say unto you, among those that are born of women there is not a greater prophet than John the Baptist; but he that is least in the Kingdom of God is greater than he."

The people who understand the time and that know that now is the time to establish the King to the kingdom are like those that came to King David years ago at Hebron.

Now, in the prophet Malachi, we see that Edom will build up, and the Lord will throw down the borders of wickedness with whom the Lord hath indignation forever. And your eyes shall see, and you shall say, "The Lord will be magnified from the border of Israel." The Lord goes on to say, "A son honors his father and a servant his master. If I be a father, where is my honor? And if I be master, where is my fear?"

In Malachi 3:13, the Lord said, "Your words have been stout against me, and you say, 'What have we spoken so much against you?'" As you go on to study this prophet, you will understand that God is not satisfied with our wounded sacrifices, only with the prefect Lamb, his sacrifice (slew from the foundations of the world), a clean sacrifice and with the firstfruits of our labor (full surrender to him). He stated that we have robbed him in tithes and offerings, therefore our blessing has been turned into a curse. But if we will repent and bring the tithe and offerings into his storehouse, He will open up the windows of heaven and pour out a blessing, that there will not be room enough to receive it, and he will rebuke the devourer for our sakes.

He also addresses our words: "For they that feared the Lord spake often one to another and the Lord hearkened and heard it, and a book of remembrance was written before Him for them that feared the Lord, and that thought upon his name. And they shall be mine, says the Lord of Hosts, in that day that I make up my jewels; and I will spare them, as a man spares his own son that serves him." Also, unto those that fear my name shall the sun of righteousness arise with healing in his wings; and you shall go forth and grow up as calves in a stall, and you shall tread down the wicked, for they shall be ashes under the soles of your feet in the day that I shall do this, says the Lord of hosts.

> Behold, I will send my messenger, and he shall prepare the way before me. And the Lord, whom you seek, shall suddenly come to his temple (you are the temple of God), even the messenger of the covenant, in whom you delight. Who may abide the day of His coming? Who shall stand when He appears? For He is like a refiner's fire and like fullers' soap. And He shall sit as a refiner and a purifier of silver and He shall purify the sons of Levi (priest) and purge them as gold and silver, that they may offer unto the Lord an offering in righteousness. (Malachi 3:1–3)

Now we are all priest unto the Lord in the new covenant, and we will all go through the fire. But do not fear, for there is one, as the Son of God, in the fire with us, and the fire will only burn off the ropes that the enemy has used to bind us. But not even the smell of smoke will be on you (Daniel 3). The Lord's fire only burns that which is for our good. He shall then use us to bind his princes and take back what the enemy has stolen.

> Let the saints be joyful in glory; let them sing aloud upon their beds. Let the high praises of God be in their mouth, and a two-edged sword on their hand. To execute vengeance upon the heathen and punishment upon the people. To bind their kings with chains, and their nobles with fetters of iron. To execute upon them the judgment written, this honor have all his saints, praise ye the Lord. (Psalm 149:5–9)

> Behold, they shall gather, together but not by me; whosoever shall gather, together against you shall fall for thy sake. Behold, I have created the smith that blows the coals in the fire, and that brings forth an instrument for his work; and I have created the waster to destroy. No weapon that is formed against you shall prosper; and every tongue that shall rise against you in judgment thou shall condemn. This is the heritage of the servants of the Lord, and their righteousness is of me, says the Lord. (Isaiah 54:15–17)

Therefore, what is left for us but to love and serve the Lord with our *whole* heart and soul, for this is the first commandment, and the second is to love thy neighbor as thyself. (Let him love through you.)

Nahum 1:7 says, "The Lord is good, a strong hold in the day of trouble and He knows them that trust Him." And I know from experience that he is well able to deliver and is ready and willing, waiting for us, like a father waits for his children to come to him.

I told you I would let you know how I know that the demons are not of this creation. One time, a friend and I decided to go out for the evening. We went to a nice restaurant in Burbank, California. And then after eating, we decided we would go to the bar. We found out that it was a club behind the restaurant. maybe she knew; I did not. And I am not sure what I expected but certainly not what I saw. When we entered, my eyes were open to another dimension, and I saw the demons dancing on the dance floor. When the people were grinding the demons were having sex. They looked more like the bar room seen in *Star Wars* than anything that exists now. I was seeing them in skeleton form. They are certainly not any creation of this world. As I stood there, not able to take my eyes off of what I was seeing, I kept hearing someone calling, "Over here by me. I saved you a place over here." I finally turned around to see where the persistent voice was coming from. And there, standing by the bar, was a gorgeous young man, a head taller than anyone else, chiseled chin, dark blond hair, waving someone over. I looked around to see who was around me, and there was no one. he pointed at me and said, "You. I saved you a place by me." I walked over, and he introduced himself. I introduced myself and asked where he was from, and he told me from the North. I asked where in the North, and he said, just far north. Then I guess I gave him an out. "Like Norway?" I asked, and he said, "Something like that." To make the long story short, I had a date with my angel. And it was a lot of fun. I do not know where my girlfriend went. I did not see her again until she came by and asked if I was ready to leave.

I want to add another thing: We talked about deceased angels having a fire in them. These demons do not. And then there are spirits that are not demons. I think they are like the fruit of the spirit. With them, it is hate, anger, bitterness, unforgiveness, and the like. These are what a few Christians call demons.

> The fruit of God's Spirit are love, joy, peace, longsuffering, gentleness, goodness, faith, meekness temperance. (Galatians 5:22–23)

I believe that just as God has fruit of the Holy Spirit, there are also fruit of the evil spirits. These need to be cleaned out and replaced with the fruit of the Holy Spirit. But these spirits are not demons. A demon has a personality like the ones that possess transgenders and the like. I once knew a lady that had several. When one is in control, the person can get along. But when there are several, and they quarrel among themselves, it makes life almost impossible for the person and for anyone around them. The medical doctors and psychiatrists have us believing this is a medical disorder, not a spiritual one, so we drug them. We cast out what is not a demon and medicate a true demon. What a deal he has going.

> Thou believes that there is one God, thou doest well; the devils also believe and tremble. (James 2:19)

Seek the Lord while he may be found, call upon Him while He is near. Let the wicked forsake his way and the unrighteous man his thoughts; and let him return unto the Lord, and He will have mercy upon him; and to our God, for He will abundantly pardon. (Isaiah 55:6–7)

Many years ago, in Los Angeles, when I was young and not walking with the Lord, a guy invited me to go with him up into the canyon because he was invited to supposedly get a reading and some drugs. Being young and curious, I went. Only God knows why. Not long after we arrived, this guy came out of the bedroom and into the living room and immediately honed in on me. "What is she doing here?" he asked. The guy answered, "You told me I could bring someone."

"She has to go," the guy said. The others there, being taken aback, began to question him. "No, she must go" was his answer, "or she can go into the bedroom with me."

"Are you willing to do that? he asked.

The answer was no.

"Well then, you have to go."

The guy I was with complained, "You said you were going to give me some drugs."

He, who I now know was a warlock, said, "Oh, you can have the drugs," and he split a tab with us then sent us out the door, knowing what would happen. He knew we would not get out of the canyon alive; but God had another plan. I remember the car going over a cliff and the fall being upside down. I called out to God, and then there was a jerk, and the car was back on the road. I remember the guy I was with saying, "What happened?" And that is about all I remember besides some lights. I woke up in my bed. Without any doubt in my mind, my angel caught the car and drove out of the canyon and on the freeways of Los Angeles, delivered me to my home, and then took the guy home as well. I know this because he was a technician at my work, and sure enough, he was back at work. I am sure the warlock looked at the news the next day to hear of the accident. And when it was not reported, he got in his car and went to look so he could be the one to report it. How disappointed he must have been that I was not dead.

If you belong to God, Satan cannot snitch you out of his hand. If God has a purpose for your life, he will fulfill it, even if you are young and stupid.

And may I say here that I do not like to have to capitalize the word Satan. I know that it is capitalized in the Bible; but it means an opponent, archenemy of good, adversary, to withstand. It is his whole kingdom, not his proper name. And in his kingdom, they will play. Will the real Satan stand up? Just know that they are all Satan. And, yes, the radical Muslims use the word correctly when they call Israel the little Satan and the United States of America the big Satan. Today, because of the way the Bible was translated, most people think of Lucifer as being Satan. And while he is one, there is a whole kingdom of Satans. We are dealing with his angels and his demons.

> Blow the trumpet in Zion and sound an alarm in my holy mountain; let all the inhabitants of the land tremble; for the day of the Lord cometh, for it is nigh at hand. A day of darkness and of gloominess, a day of clouds and of thick darkness, as the morning spread upon the

mountains, a great people and a strong; there hath not been ever the like, neither shall be any more after it. A fire devours before them; and behind them a flame burneth the land is as the garden of Eden before them, and behind them a desolate wilderness; yea, and nothing shall escape them. The appearance of them is as the appearance of horses (to skip, be rapid, leap); and as horsemen so shall they run. Like the noise of chariots on the tops of the mountains shall they leap, like the noise of a flame of fire that devoureth the stubble, a strong people set in battle array. Before their face the people shall be much pained, all faces shall gather blackness. They shall run like mighty men they shall clime the wall like men of war; and they shall march everyone on his ways, and they shall not break their ranks. Neither shall one thrust another; they shall walk everyone in his path and when they fall upon the sword, they shall not be wounded. (This tells you they are not human they are spirit; humans get wounded, what a picture of today) They shall run to and fro in the city; they shall run upon the wall, they shall climb up upon the houses; they shall enter in at the windows like a thief. (They shall enter in through the five senses) The earth shall quake before them; the heavens shall

tremble; the sun and moon shall be dark.
(Joel 2:1–13)

Now in verse 11, everything changes.

> And the Lord shall utter his voice
> before his army; for his camp is very great
> for he is strong that executeth (sends
> forth) his word; for the day of the Lord is
> great and very terrible and who can abide
> it? (He that executes his word) Therefore
> also now, saith the Lord, turn even to me
> with your heart and with fasting, and
> with weeping, and with mourning. And
> rent your heart, and not your garments
> and turn unto the Lord your God for he
> is gracious and merciful, slow to anger
> and of great kindness and repenteth (To
> turn from) him of the evil.

I will share this poem the Lord gave from the story of
Moses, who came against Pharaoh to set his people free.

The Rod of God

As Moses shepherded the flock in the desert,
he came upon something very odd
A flame of fire burning on itself, not consuming
the bush, it was the flame of God.
God called unto him Moses, Moses,
and he answered here am I
God said this ground is holy pull off
your shoes before drawing nigh.

He said, I am the God of your fathers, the God of Abraham
The God of Isaac, the God of Jacob; the great I Am.
I have seen the affliction of my people,
and I have heard their cry
By reason of their taskmasters, I know
their sorrows, and that is why.
I come to deliver them from the cruel oppression of Pharaoh
And to bring them into a good land,
of which they do not know.
Moses said, who am I that I should go? God
said, fear not, I will go with thee
And they will ask, who are you? Say
the great I Am has sent me.
I am sure that the king of Egypt will not
let go, no! But by a might hand
I have remembered my covenant, which
I made with Father Abraham.
I will rid you from Pharaoh's bondage, I
will judge them that oppress you
With my great power, I will show
wonders and plagues, not a few.
Now do not fear to speak in my name, for I have chosen you
For surely you will speak, and great wonders I will do.
For now, you shall see what I will do to Pharaoh
For with great anger and a strong hand
shall he let my people go.
The Lord said, Moses, what is that I see in your hand?
That is my shepherd's rod, a very useful tool in this land.
The Lord said, cast it on the ground,
and Moses cast it on the ground
It became a serpent, Moses fled before
it, just like we have been found.

THE DAY OF THE LORD

But the Lord said, Moses, put forth your
hand and take it by the tail
I heard Moses say, "Lord, I don't handle serpents very well."
He put forth his hand and took the serpent,
who had usurped God's power
And it became the rod of God in his
hand, so is it in this hour.

PRAYER FOR THE SPIRIT-CONTROLLED LIFE

The law of the Spirit of life in Christ Jesus has made me free from the law of sin and death. My life is governed not by the standards and according to the dictates of the flesh but controlled by the Holy Spirit. I am not living the life of the flesh; I am living the life of the Spirit. The Holy Spirit of God dwells within me and directs and controls me.

I am a conqueror and gain a surpassing victory through Jesus who loves me, and I do not let myself be overcome by evil but overcome and master evil with good. I have on the full armor of light. I cloth myself with the Lord Jesus Christ, the Messiah, and make no provision for indulging the flesh.

I am a doer of God's Word, and I have God's wisdom. I am peace loving, courteous, considerate, gentle, willing to yield to reason, full of compassion and good fruits. I am free from doubts, wavering, and insincerity; I am subject to God.

As I have received Christ Jesus, the Lord, so I walk in Him, rooted and built up in him, and established in the faith. I stand firm against the devil. I resist the devil, and he will flee from me. I come close to God, and God comes close to me. I do not fear, for God will never leave me or forsake me.

In Christ, I am filled with the Godhead: Father, Son, and Holy Spirit. Jesus is my Lord.

Scripture references:

- Romans 8:2, 4, 9, 14, 31, 37
- Romans 12:21
- Romans 13:12, 14
- James 1:22
- James 3:17
- Hebrews 13:5
- James 4:7–8
- Colossians 2:6–7, 9–10

WHAT TIME IS IT?

Really, what time is it? The word *history* really says "his story." I suggest that this is no coincidence, since all this creation has been about him and his taking back the kingdom and restoring all things back to the Father after the rebellion of one of his created angels.

We have been familiar with looking at a clock with a midnight hour on it and the hands at shortly before midnight. This has led us to think that Jesus is coming back in the midnight hour. But God is not on our calendar or our time. God is on the Hebrew calendar and Hebrew time. In Hebrew time, a day is from sundown to sundown. As in the creation, God said the evening and the morning were the first day, and the evening and the morning were the second day, and the evening and the morning were the third day, etc. Time was created by God at that time and is only for us here and now; only this creation is in time. In Revelation 10:6, we find that there should be time no longer. If we begin to look at time the same way God does, it may help us better understand his word.

God's months are different also, given to the Hebrew children. They are all on a lunar cycle, taking a part of two of our months. His new year, Rosh Hashanah, will be in the month of Tishri (first month civil year and seventh month of sacred year) and usually starts somewhere between midmonth and the end of September. And their holidays change each year, based on the new moon. And this must be witnessed by two witnesses and reported to the priest. And then the priest come out of the temple and begin to sound the seven trumpets. Sounds a bit like in the book of Revelation, yes. Next will come the holiest day on the Jewish calendar, Yom Kippur, the Day of Atonement, when they fast and pray and seek God's forgiveness. On this Day of Atonement, "Aaron shall offer his bullock of the sin offering, which is for himself and make an atonement for himself and for his house. And he shall take the two goats and present them before the Lord at the door of the tabernacle of the congregation. And Aaron shall cast lots upon the two goats; one lot for the Lord, and the other lot for the scapegoat" (goat of removal, Azazel). And Aaron shall bring the goat upon which the Lord's lot fell and offer him for a sin offering (representing Jesus). But the goat, on which the lot fell to be the scapegoat, shall be presented alive before the Lord to make an atonement with him and to let him go for a scapegoat into the wilderness (Leviticus 16:6–10).

> And he is the propitiation (make amends, appease) for our sins, and not for ours's only (who have received him) but also for the sins of the whole world. (Those still under the government of Azazel, in the wilderness.) (1 John 2:2)

After this, five days later, we come to tabernacles, seven days where the people tabernacle with the Lord living in booths, temporary housing, depicting the seven days. We are here in this time, living in temporary bodies, tabernacling with God.

Time is an element created by God, at the creation, to house this creation, and keep the darkness of this world from spreading to other universes. Many have spent hours, trying to understand prophecy according to our time, not God's time, not taking into consideration what God said that all was finished before the foundations of this creation. God being outside of time just looks and sees his Word coming to pass in time, as he already has finished it outside of time. And outside of time, it is all there. Those in Old Testament times that moved into the new covenant before Christ came, just looked forward to the Messiah the same way you and I look back to the events of Calvary. What is necessary is for us to get through the veil of angelic authority to understand what God has always understood. Second Corinthians 3:12–17 says that we can use great plainness of speech, not as Moses, which put a veil over his face that the children of Israel could not look to the end of that which is abolished. But their minds were blinded, for until this day remains the same veil untaken away in the reading of the Old Testament; which veil is done away in Christ. Even unto this day, when Moses is read, the veil is upon their heart. Nevertheless, when you shall turn to the Lord, the veil shall be taken away. Although this is true, we still find many of God's people on this side of the veil, having great theological discussions. God has already finished his work and is waiting for us to move into the finished work with him.

At the time, Jesus hung his head and gave up the spirit, the veil between the most holy place and the holy place in the temple was rent from the top to the bottom (Matthew 27:51). We can consider that the temple is in three parts, depicting the three parts of man's spirit, soul, and body. And the veil was rent, allowing God to come out and into our spirits and occupy our spirits, souls, and bodies. Just as importantly is the earth and its cosmos, with its dark forces in rule, being the first heaven, the heavens connected to our earth, the second heaven being other universes, where God's unfallen angels rule, and the third heaven being God's throne or the most holy place. God rent the veil of angelic authority, stripped the fallen angels of their authority, and gave that authority back to his new sons. He planted a son that he might bring many sons into glory; that to as many as received him, he gave authority to become the sons of God (John 1:12). The inner veil was made of blue, purple, and scarlet and of fine-twined linen of cunning work with cherubim on it (Exodus 26:31) and the temple also (2 Chronicles 3:14). These cherubim depict the cherubim that kept the way of the tree of life. At the cross, their power was broken. Man could now eat of the tree of life and live.

God, being outside of time, is watching us as we make our choices, much like you might watch a play. He already knows your choice. He wrote the play, did the casting, carried the heavy part himself, and wrote the conclusion all before he created man.

In Mark 6:45–52, we find Mark's version of the story when Jesus came to the disciples, walking on the water. Jesus could just as easily have planned this day any other way. We could think he has a message to his children in the way he set up this day. He had just fed the five thousand with five loaves and two fish, and now he sent the disciples in a boat to the other side, and he went up into a mountain to pray. He saw them toiling in rowing because the wind was contrary unto them. And in the fourth watch of the night, he came to them, walking on the water, and would have passed by them had they not cried out to him. Then He said, "Be of good cheer. It is I. Be not afraid." We can see the similarity of Jesus sending the church on the Great Commission and going back to sit at the right hand of the Father, where he is always interceding for us and watching over us, He knew when the winds are contrary, and he can see our toiling and our progress. John said in his version of this story that they had rowed about twenty-five or thirty furlongs, which is about three to three and one-half miles. This is not very far, considering they were already in the fourth and last watch just before dawn. When the night was the darkest, coldest, and the scariest, this is when Jesus decided to walk by but would have passed them by had they not cried out to him.

The scripture says the disciples were amazed when the winds ceased and considered not the miracle of the loaves. We at times seem also not to be able to believe that he is able to handle whatever comes into our lives. Jesus is always there, waiting for us to call out to him. And when we do, the winds, which are against us, will yield to us who speak and believe his word. I like the part which John added to this story, which the other writers did not, and that is that as soon as they, Jesus and Peter, had entered the ship, immediately the ship was at the land where they were going. We can also learn from this story that all our toil, without Jesus, will not get us were we are going. It is only as we cry out to him that he comes to our assistance. And at that time, nothing is impossible. There will be a time when Jesus has been willingly received into our ship that we, too, will find that immediately we will be at our destination.

Next, let us look at Matthew's version of this story. He recorded Peter's part in the story. Peter answered, "Lord, if it be you, bid (ask or command) me to come unto you on the water." Jesus said, "*Come!*" And Peter got out of the ship and walked on the water to go to Jesus. You and I will never go out to meet Jesus unless we are willing to take the chance Peter took. Oh, yes, you will be saved, as the other disciples in the ship were saved, and get to your destination, heaven. The boldness and willingness of Peter in asking to come to Jesus is to be appreciated though, while all of the disciples were of different personalities, which shows us that he can and will use every one from doubting Thomas to impetuous Peter, who usually spoke before he thought. Some may relate and say, "I need a slower tongue or a faster brain," but on the other hand, some of us think too long and move too slowly. This is why, which ever type we are, we all must surrender to the working of Christ in our personalities. We know that Peter did walk on the water to Jesus, as long as he kept his eyes on Jesus and not on the boisterous winds. It is when Peter looked at the boisterous winds (the circumstances) that he became afraid and that fear caused him to sink. And when he cried out to the Lord, the Lord saved him. But did Peter walk on the water or on the Word of Jesus? Remember, he asked Jesus to "bid me come to you," and Jesus said, "*Come.*" Peter could not have done the impossible without the Word of Jesus. He walked on the word *come*. If Jesus had not said come, Peter could not have walked himself on the water. But with the Word of God, all things are possible.

In Matthew 25:1–13, we have the parable of the ten virgins. All were virgins. All had lamps and oil. But the difference is the five wise virgins took oil in their vessels with their lamps. While the bridegroom tarried, they all slumbered and slept. But at midnight, there was a cry made, "Behold, the bridegroom cometh. Go out to meet him." Now this is what happens at midnight: There was a mighty move of God in the infilling of the Holy Spirit (oil in vessels) and a cry "the bridegroom cometh. Go out to meet him." The five foolish virgins are the ones with no oil in their vessels, and it appears that oil is not something that you can borrow. You must get it through an infilling of the Holy Spirit. Now is the time for such an outworking. Today begins that walk with God and let him have his way in your life, lest he comes and says, "I never knew you."

Second Peter 1:19 says, "We have also a more, sure word of prophecy; whereunto you do well that you take heed, as unto a light that shines in a dark place, until the day dawn, and the day star arise in your hearts." Now the day star, sometimes called the morning star, is the star that shines in the darkest part of the night, just before dawn, in the fourth watch.

Just as a star announced the first coming, so a star announces the second coming. But not everyone saw or noticed the star in the sky at Jesus's first coming, so not everyone can or will see the day star. And he arise in their hearts. However, there are some that know his touch and the quiver in their spirit is like unto a bride's quiver at the anticipation of the bridegroom's touch.

Remember the call, "go out to meet Him"? Well, this is very much what Peter did in getting out of the ship and walking on his Word to him, for those who have ears to hear, hear the call *come, awake*, and be not afraid to step out on God's Word. Remember, his Word will not fail you, and he is not a man that will lie. It is impossible for God to lie (Hebrews 6:18). Let every man be a liar, but God's Word be true. Romans 3:3–4 says, "For what if some did not believe? Shall their unbelief make the faith of God without effect? God forbid, yea, let God be true but every man a liar." God cannot lie because if he speaks, the breath of God, the spirit goes forth and preforms his word.

> So shall my word be that goes forth
> out of my mouth, it shall not return unto
> me void; but it shall accomplish that

> which I please, and it shall prosper in the
> thing whereto I sent it. (Isaiah 55:11)

This means that if you return his word to him, he will surely perform that word. So many do not understand how to pray today and set about to pray from their own understanding instead of just praying his Word.

Job said, "Oh that one would hear me behold my desire is, that the Almighty would answer me, and that mine adversary had written a book. Surely, I would take it upon my shoulder and bind it as a crown to me. I would declare unto him the number of my steps; as a prince would I go near unto him" (Job 31:35–37). And God answered Jobs prayer and gave a book. Today we call that book the Bible. And in Job 19:23, it says, "Oh that my words were now written, oh that they were printed in a book." And God said, "I can do that also." Today Job is part of the Bible.

You can see that God needed a man in this realm to petition him for his written word, just as he needed a man in Abraham's day to believe that he was able to give the promised son and accounted that God was able to raise him up even from the dead (Hebrews 11:19). God has limited himself to work through his man that he created for this purpose, not because he must but because he has chosen to. He desires a family.

> I Jesus have sent mine angel to tes-
> tify unto you these things in the churches.
> I am the root and the offspring of David,
> the bright, and morning star. (Revelation
> 22:16)

> He that overcomes and keeps my
> works unto the end, to him will I give

> power over the nations; and he shall rule
> them with a rod of iron; as the vessel of
> a potter shall they be broken to shivers;
> even as I received of my Father; and I will
> give him the morning star, he that hath
> an ear, let him hear what the Spirit says
> unto the churches. (Revelation 2:26–29)

His desire is a people that will surrender to him and let him have his way in and through them to take back dominion of this earth, which we lost to the darkness in the beginning in the garden. God has delivered us from the power, authority of darkness, and hath translated us into the kingdom of his dear Son (Colossians 1:13).

> For by him were all things created,
> that are in heaven and that are in earth,
> visible and invisible; whither they be
> thrones or dominions or principalities
> or powers all things were created by him
> and for him. And he is before all things,
> and by him all things consist. And he is
> the head of the body, the church, who
> is the beginning the first born from the
> dead, that in all things he might have the
> preeminence... It is Christ in you the
> hope of glory. (verses 16–18, 27)

> We have this treasure in earthen vessels, that the excellence of the power may
> be of God and not of us. (2 Corinthians
> 4:7)

GOD'S PLAN FOR YOU

And God spoke all these words: "I am the Lord thy God, which have brought you out of the land of Egypt, out of the house of bondage. You shall not have any other gods but me because I, the Lord thy God, am a jealous God" (paraphrased).

What does God mean by "I am a jealous God"?

First, we need to understand ourselves and our part in God's plan. Why are we here, and what is our purpose? We are here to replace the rebellious sons of God in the divine council.

God, speaking to Lucifer, said, "You have sinned, therefore I will cast thee as profane out of the mountain of God and from the midst of the stones of fire. Your heart was lifted up because of your beauty. You have corrupted your wisdom by reason of thy brightness. I will cast you to the ground. I will lay you before kings that they may behold you. You have defiled your sanctuaries (a palace or dwelling place of a deity, whether Jehovah or of idols) by the multitude of your iniquities (pervert or perversity to do wrong—i.e., go against God, your Creator), by the iniquity of thy traffic. Therefore will I bring forth a fire from the midst of you, (note: where the fire is coming from) it shall devour you and I will bring you to ashes upon the earth in the sight of all them that behold you."

NOW IS THE TIME

Between Genesis 1:1 and 1:2, something had happened to God's original creation, which had destroyed the earth and brought darkness upon his creation. This was that an angel, namely Lucifer, the prince of Tyrus, of whom we are told was a covering cherub by the prophet Ezekiel in chapter 28, verses 12 through 16.

> Son of man, take up a lamentation upon the king of Tyrus (to cover over) and say unto him, Thus says the Lord God; you sealed up the sum, full of wisdom, and perfect in beauty. You have been in Eden the garden of God; every precious stone was thy covering the sardius, topaz, and the diamond, the beryl, the onyx, and the jasper, the sapphire, the emerald, and the carbuncle, (this list most of the stones in the foundation of the new Jerusalem) the gold; the workmanship of thy tabrets and of thy pipes was prepared in thee in the day that you were created.

Notice, he was also created as a musical being, probably why he has taken over our music in these last days. Hitler used the 440 Hz. and got the United States and Canada to change all instruments to be tuned to 440 Hz. This being a frequency that shatters the spirit of man, so the dark forces can better control man, and he has us trying to worship God with this music. Going on...

> Thou art the anointed cherub that covers and I have set thee, you were upon the holy mountain of God you

101

have walked up and down in the midst,
of the stones of fire. You were perfect in
thy ways from the day that you were created, till iniquity was found in you. By
the multitude of thy merchandise (trade
or traffic) has filled the midst of you with
violence.

God plan is to use his man. Satan was quite upset, no
doubt, that God had given the control of his former kingdom to these new beings. If you ever had any doubts as to
what Satan thinks of you, don't doubt any longer. Be assured
that he hates you and will do anything he can to destroy
you. You might be saying, "I don't think that is a very good
plan." Would anyone, faced with the problem of a rebellious
angel, with an army of fellow angels, choose such a weak
creation with which to win the battle? I believe Satan's sides
were hurting from laughing. Well, remember that God has
said, "My ways are not your ways."

I, the Lord thy God, am a jealous God. You shall not
have any other gods but me. God would not need to say this
unless there was another who was trying to deceive us into
thinking they were god or that we ourselves were gods apart
from God.

The word Baal #1166 in *Strong's Exhaustive Concordance
of the Bible* means "to be master, to marry, have dominion
over, be husband." Likewise, let us look at Adonay #136. It
is an emphatic name for the Lord, meaning God only or my
Lord, taken from #113 Adon, meaning to rule sovereign,
controller, lord, master, owner, much the same as Baal. *El*
#410 means mighty and almighty, used also as a deity, God
or little god, great, idol, mighty, strong. While Elohim #430
is plural for El. It can mean gods in the ordinary sense, as

well as the Supreme God, can mean magistrates, and sometimes as a superlative angel. And Jehovah or Yehovah #3068 means the self-existent or eternal, the name of the God of Israel. The Most High is Elyown, the one Lucifer wanted to be like. So, with all these words being used as one word in English for God, you might see how, when you read the Bible, many are confused. You will see that Baal and Adonay have almost the same meaning. This is because Satan wants the same pace in your life that was created for God alone. You might also notice that Baal worship is not a thing of the past.

Jehovah or Yehovah is the self-existent, the beginning and the end, Alpha and Omega, which is, which was, and which is to come the Almighty. Nothing we do adds to him, and nothing we do can take away from him (Revelation 1:8). In Yehovah is everything that exists, has ever existed, or will exist in the future. Satan, being an angel and created by Yehovah, is still using Yehovah's power against him since Satan has no power of his own, only what was given to him by Yehovah. And Paul said in Romans 11:29, "The gifts and calling of God are without repentance," meaning that God does not change his mind and take them back. (This explains Saul and David and how David treated Saul.) This explains why so many things happen in this world that we just don't seem to be able to explain, like all the bad things that happen to seemly good people and why God gets the blame for it all, when really, God is not the one doing the evil. We are told in 1 Samuel 15:23 that rebellion is as the sin of witchcraft, and stubbornness is as iniquity and idolatry. Witchcraft is simply using God's power in rebellion against him, and Baal or idol worship is letting any spirit, apart from Yehovah, have dominion over us and thereby produce offspring to that spirit, like a wife to a husband as God, our

Adonay, is our husband, and we are to produce life for him. Our souls, the womb of God, will either produce life for God or death for Satan, and we give birth through our words.

> Death and life are in the power of the tongue and keep thy heart with all diligence for out of it are the issues of life.
> (Proverbs 18:21; 4:23)

James 1:14–15 tells us how Satan uses the same womb to produce his seed as God does. Everyone is tempted when he is drawn away of his own lust (ovum) and enticed. Then when lust hath conceived, it bringeth forth sin; and sin, when it is finished, bringeth forth death.

Now Yehovah is, and we can do nothing to add to Yehovah. And we do nothing that will take away from Yehovah. He is the All-Existent. But Adonay is something we make Yehovah when we acknowledge his lordship. The first time it appears in the Bible is in Genesis 15:1–2. Yehovah told Abram, "I am thy shield and thy exceeding great reward." And Abram said, "Adonay Yehovah, what will you give me, seeing I go childless, having not seed in the world?" Abram was acknowledging Yehovah's lordship. Each one that acknowledges Yehovah's lordship (making him Lord (Adonay) of your life) has regained connection, power, and blessings from Yehovah. We find that *Adonay* was used when He was addressing Israel and by Abraham and many of the prophets of Israel when they are addressing Yehovah. Yehovah becomes Adonay to us when we acknowledge his lordship, and it is Adonay that will judge his people; all others will be judged by Yehovah, since evil is now existing in Yehovah, existing in the form of Satan and his angels, until they are done away with, Yehovah declares in Isaiah 54:16, "Behold,

I have created the smith that bloweth the coals in the fire, and that bringeth forth an instrument for his work and I have created the waster to destroy." He will use Satan and his followers to destroy his followers, and then Yehovah will destroy Satan himself with the sword of His mouth. There is a great fire in evil that destroys. And since spirit exists forever, the fire will burn forever. Isaiah 27 speaks of destroying leviathan with his sword. In verse 4, he says, "Fury is not in me." He asked, "Who would make battle with me? But rather let him take hold of my strength and make peace with me." He said he would cause Israel to take root, blossom, and bear fruit. And then the Lord asked, "Hath he smitten him as he smote those that smote him (in reaction), or is he slain according to the slaughter of them that are slain by him? It is the latter; he just is reaping what he has sown. We reap what we sow, and God does not have to punish anyone. Evil will reap death. It is built into the laws of the universe, just as assuredly as gravity.

In Genesis 14:16, God told Abram that it would be four generations before his children would be able to inherit the land because the iniquity of the Amorites was not yet full. The Amorites had to fill up their cup of iniquity, then judgment would come on them. In Revelation 17, we see the woman, Mystery Babylon, THE GREAT MOTHER OF THE HARLOTS AND ABOMINATIONS OF THE EARTH, with this cup in her hand. And in chapter 18, verse 6, "Reward her even as she rewarded you and double unto her double according to her works, in the cup which she hath filled, fill to her double."

God is an Elohim, a spirit being, but no other Elohim is like him. He is one of a kind. He alone is the perfect sovereign Creator, God with a capital G, the Most High. In John 3:16, it says, "For God so loved the world, that he gave his only begotten Son, that whosoever believeth in him should not perish, but have everlasting life." He is also one of a kind, a unique son, as was the son of the promise. Remember the word *yachad*, to unite into one son. Jesus is one with the Father and with the Spirit, making the trinity. The angels being created by him are not one with him but are to be his imagers in heaven as humans are to be his imagers on earth. But Lucifer and one-third of the sons of God in the heavens and man on the earth have both failed. Thus, God's plan to become a man and to rectify the results of sin. The angels desire to investigate this.

> What is man that thou art mindful of him? And the son of man, that thou visitest him? For thou hast made him a little lower than the angels, and hast crowed with glory and honor. Thou makest him to have dominion over the works of thy hands; thou hast put all things under his feet. (Psalm 8:4–6)

Man's job was to make all the earth like the garden of Eden.

Now let us go to Genesis 11 where we find the people building a city and a tower, probably led by Nimrod. They said, "Let us make bricks." Why would you want to make bricks in a land covered by rock? Well, rocks are individual, and brick are all the same uniform, easier to work with or control, a communist thing. In verse 6, it says, "And the Lord said behold the people are one (one accord) and they have one language, now nothing will be restrained form them, which they have imagined doing." God confused their language and scattered them abroad upon the face of the earth.

Deuteronomy speaks of when God did this.

> When the Most High gave to
> the nations their inheritance, when he
> divided mankind, he fixed the borders of
> the peoples according to the number of
> the sons of God. But the LORD's portion
> is his people, Jacob his allotted heritage.
> (Deuteronomy 32:8–9 ESV)

God gave the nations to the sons of God, the angels, small gods. In the King James version and Bibles translated from manuscripts of that time, it says children of Israel. But in the Dead Sea Scrolls discovered since that time, it says sons of God, which would seem to be true since there was not at that time a nation of Israel in existence. However, God knew his plan was to pick Abram and start a new nation for himself. He went on to speak of how Israel, his people, had not walked in his ways. And in Deuteronomy 32:26–27 ESV, it says, "I would have said, 'I will cut them to pieces; I will wipe them from human memory,' had I not feared provocation by the enemy, lest their adversaries should misunderstand, lest they should say, 'Our hand is triumphant, it was not the LORD who did all this.'" God was saying the enemy, the rebellious sons of God, would think they had triumphed and that he had given up on Israel, which he would not do; they understand nothing. They walked about in darkness; all the foundations of the earth are shaken. I said, "You are gods. You are all sons of the Most High, but you will die like mere mortals. You will fall like every other ruler. Rise up, O God. Judge the earth, for all the nations are your inheritance." God's plan is to take back the nations.

At that time, Jacob was his allotted heritage. All the nations were given to the rebellious sons of God, and only Israel was the Lord's heritage. And Job 15:15 says that God places no trust in his holy ones, even the heavens are not pure in his eyes.

> For the indignation of the Lord is upon all nations, and his Fury upon all their armies; he hath utterly destroyed them, he hath delivered them to the slaughter. And all the host of heaven shall be dissolved, and the heavens shall be rolled together as a scroll; and all their host shall fall down, as the leaf falleth off from the vine, and as a falling fig from the fig tree. (Isaiah 34:2, 4)

I want to go to verse 5 because Idumea is the name given to Edom.

> For my sword shall be bathed in heaven behold, it shall come down upon Idumea and upon the people of my curse, to judgment.

These are the people of Edom mixed with Seir, spoken about earlier in this book.

Edom was taken by Babylon around 600 BC and pushed into Judea. When the Greeks took over, they changed their name to Idumea.

> Isaiah 24:21 It shall come to pass in that day, that the Lord shall punish the

host of the high ones that are on high,
and the kings of the earth upon the
earth. God will punish both the high
ones, rulers in the heavens; and the kings
of the earth, that have worked for them
on the earth.

Jacob was the Lord's allotted heritage. This is known as
cosmic geography in 2 Kings 5 in the time of Elisha. There
was a man named Naaman, who was the captain of the king
of Syria's armies, and he had leprosy. The army had brought a
little handmaid from Israel, and she waited on Naaman. She
told him that the God of Israel would heal him and that he
should go to the prophet of Israel. Naaman and his servants
went to Israel to Elisha, and Elisha told him to go wash in the
Jordan. Naaman was not pleased with this. He had wanted
the prophet to come and meet him as he was an important
person, but his servant convinced him to go and wash. And
when he did, he was healed. He went back to the prophet
and said in verse 15b, "Now I know that there is no God in
all the earth, but in Israel, now therefore, I pray thee take a
blessing of thy servant." Verse 17 says, "And Naaman said,
shall there not then, I pray thee, be given to thy servant two
mules burden of earth? For thy servant will henceforth offer
neither burnt offering nor sacrifice unto other gods, but unto
the Lord." Naaman understood that the nations about worshipped other gods, and he wanted soil from God's inheritance on which to worship.

We, as Israel after the spirit, his habitation in the earth,
are to surrender to his Holy Spirit. And when we do, we
too become holy ground and, under his direction, take our
place as the rulers of this earth as this was restored to us by
Jesus's death and undoing of the powers of darkness by his

resurrection. Satan is already a defeated foe. Jesus defeated him and won a judgement. But with a judgement, you still must collect on it. When we accept the proposal of Adonay to make him the Lord of our lives, begin to produce life unto him, making him the King of our life. He gives us a position greater than we could ever imagine. To Him be glory, honor, and power forever and ever.

First Kings 22:19–22 tells us how the sons of God in the council consulted with God on how to get rid of Ahab when he had filled up his cup of wickedness. The prophet Micaiah said, "Hear thou therefore the word of the Lord. I saw the Lord sitting on his throne and all the host of heaven standing by him on his right hand and on his left." And the Lord said, "Who will persuade Ahab that he may go up and fall at Ramoth-Gilead?" And one said on this manner, and another said on that manner. And there came forth a spirit and stood before the Lord and said, "I will persuade him." And the Lord said unto him, "Wherewith?" And he said, "I will go forth, and I will be a lying spirit in the mouth of all his prophets," and he said, "Thou shalt persuade him and prevail also, go forth and do so."

> The Lord said unto Satan, behold all that he hath is in thy power; only upon himself put not forth thy hand. (Job 1:12)

> For the Lord is a great God, and a great King above all gods. (Psalm 95:3)

> For the Lord is great, and greatly to be praised; he is to be feared above all gods. (Psalm 96:4)

Confounded be all they that serve graven images, that boast themselves of idols; worship him, all ye gods. For thou, Lord, art high above all the earth; thou art exalted for above all gods. (Psalm 97:7, 9)

O give thanks unto the God of gods; for his mercy endures forever. (Psalm 136:2)

Who is like unto thee, O Lord (Yehovah) among the gods (Elohim) who is like thee, glorious in holiness, fearful in praises doing wonders? (Exodus 15:11)

And the king said unto her (the witch) Be not afraid, for what sawest thou? And the woman said unto Saul, I saw gods (Elohim, this one is a disembodied spirit, known as a familiar spirit) ascending out of the earth. (1 Samuel 28:13)

Lest ye lift up thine eyes unto heaven and see the sun, moon and stars, and all the host of heaven and worship them and serve them, which the Lord thy God hath divided unto all nations under the whole heaven. (Deuteronomy 4:19 paraphrased)

That should be enough to show the validity. Now, in Daniel 10:12–13, we see that the angel Gabriel was on his way to the nation of Persia to cause Daniel to understand, "but the prince (Paul called it principalities) of the kingdom of Persia withstood me twenty-one days, but Michael, one of the chief princes, came to help me and remains there with the kings of Persia." Gabriel and Michael, both God's good princes, were forces to fight with the fallen princes or rebellious sons of God.

This reminds me to talk about King David and King Saul. Both were anointed by the same prophet, Samuel. You might ask that if God knew that Saul would fail him, why would he anoint him? God also knew Adam and Eve would fail, but he gave his children, free will. God has free will, and we were made in his image to be imagers of him. Without free will, we would not be imagers. So the two kingdoms of Saul and David reflect the two kingdoms of this earth that we are now in: the kingdom of Satan and the kingdom of the Son of God, Jesus. Which is why we say, "The year of our Lord." Saul was jealous of David and sought to kill him, just like Satan hates Jesus and us. We are the feet and toes of Daniel's statue's clay and iron that do not mix. We are the clay pots with the life of Christ in us (Colossians 1:27), and the iron is the residue of the Roman kingdom, still in the beast system.

To help us understand, here are a few verses from the New Testament:

> For we all beholding as in a glass
> the glory of the Lord, are changed into
> the same image from glory to glory, even
> by the Spirit of the Lord. (2 Corinthians
> 3:18 paraphrased)

As we have born the image of the earthy, we shall also bear the image of the heavenly. (1 Corinthians 15:49)

Who (speaking of Christ) is the image of the invisible God the firstborn of every creature. (Colossians 1:15)

Verses 16 and 17 tell us that he created all things.

He is the head of the body, the church (called out ones, us); who is the beginning, the firstborn from the dead; that in all things he might have the pre-eminence. (Most outstand worth or rank) (verse 18)

And put on the new man, which is renewed in knowledge after the image of him that created him. (Colossians 3:10)

Behold, what manner of love the Father hath bestowed upon us, that we should be called the sons of God; there-fore, the world knoweth us not, because it knew him not. Beloved, now are we the sons of God, and it doth not yet appear what we shall be; but we know that, when he shall appear, we shall be like him; for we shall see him as he is. (1 John 3:1–2)

> Because you are sons, God has sent
> forth the spirit of his Son into your hearts
> crying Abba, Father. (Galatians 4:6)

> The Spirit itself bears witness with
> our spirit, that we are the children of God
> and heirs and joint heirs with Christ.
> (Romans 8:16–17)

The knowledge that all humans are representatives of God prompts us to see all human life as sacred, equal imagers of God, and leaves no room for racism, injustice. And the abuse of power has no place and cannot be justified. The choice to give his children free will has been costly to God, as both his supernatural and his earthly children have rebelled. Yet God wanted a family like himself that he could have a relationship with, not because he needs it but because he wanted it.

Satan's kingdom was expecting the Son of God to show up, but they were not sure when and what he was going to do. In the temptation in the wilderness, as recorded by Matthew and Luke, Satan asked with two of the temptation, "*If you are the Son of God,*" temping him to reveal who he was and to move from the Son of God instead of the Son of Man. And the third time, he wanted Jesus to worship him, offering all the kingdoms of the world. In Matthew 8:29, when Jesus was casting out the demons, they cried out, "What have we to do with thee, Jesus, thou Son of God? Art, thou come hither to torment us before the time?" stating they knew there was a time of judgment. And in 1 Corinthians 2:8, it says, "None of the princes of this world (age) knew; for had they known it, they would not have crucified the Lord of glory." Their biggest victory was their undoing. God outsmarted them.

Once again, they are expecting something to happen and are starting to prepare the masses to expect the aliens, the outer space type, as before long the princes in the heavens will be cast out. They have their cover story and are prepared to deceive the masses of the people.

Remember the tower of Babel spoken of earlier, where God confused their languages in Acts 2:5-11? We find God's remedy for this when the Holy Spirit filled the people, and they began to speak in tongues. The people were all amazed and marveled as they heard these Galileans speaking in their own language. All the known languages were at Jerusalem at that time. This is probably why Paul, apostle to the gentiles, wanted to push on to Spain (Romans 15:24, 28) then known as Tarshish, to cover what was the far reaches of the then-known world with the gospel. Many believe today that tongues are just for you to speak to God and to build up yourself. First Corinthians 13:1 says that though I speak with the tongues of men and of angels, I can tell you that in spiritual warfare. I have had my tongues changed to speak to angels over different countries, and you can tell and know, as the language changes and the authority changes. Spiritual warfare is probably the most important reason for tongues, speaking in the name of Yeshua under the power of the Holy Spirit. And in their own language, we have the victory. And Ephesians 6:12 says that principalities and powers and the rulers of darkness of this world must bow and obey. Paul understood this and knew who his enemy was as he took the gospel to the then-known world.

We know from Daniel 10:13,20–21 that there are princes over counties. There are also princes over states and cities. Large cities, such as Los Angeles, have many different areas, and each has its own angel over that area (city of lost angels). There are also angels over governments, education, media, and churches, just to name a few. And we should be battling each as God leads. Judges 4 and 5 tells of the battle of Deborah and Barak. And in chapter 5, verse 23, it says, "Curse ye Meroz, said the angel of the Lord, curse ye bitterly the inhabitants thereof; because they came not to the help of the Lord, to the help of the Lord against the mighty."

I wish to make another observation from Judges 5. Deborah said, "Hear, O ye kings give ear, O ye princes. I will sing unto the Lord; I will sing praise to the Lord God of Israel." Here, let me say that this battle was between Mt. Carmel and Mt. Tabor and extended down to Megiddo, in the middle of the Jezreel Valley. Now hear the word of the prophetess. "Lord, when thou went out of Seir (he-goat devil), when you march out of the field of Edom (the flesh), the earth trembled, and the heavens dropped. The clouds also dropped water." The mountains melted from before the Lord, even Sinai (the law, world system) from before the Lord God of Israel. Let me put forth that she was speaking to the kings and princes of the heavens and that she prophesied to them. Seir and Edom are down below the Dead Sea, and Sinai is even farther away in the Sinai desert; none of these places have anything to do with this war. She prophesied to them and spoke of the devil, the flesh and the world system all bowing before the presence of the Lord God of Israel.

And at that time shall Michael stand up, the great prince which stands for the children of thy people; and there shall be a time of trouble, such as never was since there was a nation even to that same time and at that time thy people shall be delivered, everyone that shall be found written in the book. (Daniel 12:1)

Revelation 12:7–12 says it this way: "And there was war in heaven; Michael and his angels fought against the dragon; and the dragon fought and his angels and prevailed not; neither was their place found any more in heaven. The great dragon was cast out, (note when he is cast out), that old serpent, called the Devil and Satan which deceived the whole world; he was cast out into the earth and his angels were cast out with him." He was cast out of the courts of heaven and God's council when the blood was brought into the heavenly mercy seat. But he is still ruling in the first heaven, the cosmos that is with our earth even now but not for too much longer. You might quote me the verse that says I saw Satan fall from heaven. Just remember, he is outside of time, and God sees everything from the end to beginning. Yes, he goes from right to left. Continuing with verse 10, "And I heard a loud voice saying in heaven, now is come salvation and strength, and the kingdom of our God and the power of his Christ; for the accuser of our brethren is cast down, which accused them before our God, day and night. And they overcame him by the blood of the Lamb, and by the word of their testimony, and they loved not their lives unto the death. Therefore, rejoice, ye heavens and ye that dwell in them. Woe to the inhibitors of the earth and of the sea for the devil is come down unto you, having great wrath because he knoweth that he hath but a short time." I believe that we go up when he comes down. We take their place as the rulers of this world. We are here to replace the rebellious sons of God in the divine council.

> I beheld till the thrones were cast
> down and the Ancient of days did sit,
> whose garment was white as snow, and
> the hair of his head like the pure wool;

> his throne was like the fiery flame, and
> his wheels as burning fire. I beheld and
> the same horn made war with the saints
> and prevailed against them; until the
> Ancient of days came. And judgment was
> given to the saints of the Most High; and
> the time came that the *saints possessed the*
> *kingdom.* (Daniel 7:9, 21–22)

You can see that the kingdom is now, but we have not taken possession yet. We have not collected on our judgment (forced them to pay up) that Yeshua obtained for us; we have not made his enemies his footstool.

> And he that overcomes and keeps
> my works, unto the end, to him will I
> give power over the nations; and he shall
> rule them with a rod of iron; as the ves-
> sels of a potter shall they be broken to
> shivers; even as I received of my father.
> (Revelation 2:26–27)

> Jesus says, my Father worketh and
> hitherto, and I work. (John 5:17)

And I say, his sons will work also in their father's busi-ness; it is a family business. And John 6:29 says, "This is the work of God, that you believe on him whom he hath sent." Belief is counted as faith, and faith is counted as righteousness.

> Thou art worthy, O Lord, to receive
> glory and honor and power for thou

hast created all things and for thy pleasure they are and were (I am) created.
(Revelation 4:11)

I am going to take a little liberty with the scriptures here
as shown to me by the Holy Spirit.

And when He had opened the seventh seal there was silence in heaven for
about a space of half an hour (however
long that is in heaven). (Revelation 8:1)

I asked God what was happening at that time; this is
what I got: When He had opened the seventh seal, there was
silence in heaven for about a space of half an hour. As the
angels and all creation were in awe, all read what my Lord
had written. I saw my name written there. He called me a
son. He called me an heir. He left me an inheritance in a far-
away country, a land that had been plundered by an enemy.
And His word to me, that His will be done: "Bring this land
into the kingdom of my dear Son."

I fell at his feet to worship him, and
he said unto me, see thou do it not; I am
thy fellow servant and of thy brethren
that have the testimony of Jesus, worship God for the testimony of Jesus is the
Spirit of prophecy. (Revelation 19:10)

Prophecy is his, Jesus's, story or testimony. And a testimony is also a will. He has written his will in his testimony
and left it for us. The testimony of Jesus is the spirit of proph-

ecy. To understand prophecy, we must have his Spirit. And with His Spirit, we will understand his story.

Now for a will or testimony to be in effect, there must first be the death of the testator. For this reason, he came and died that we might inherit.

> The eyes of our understanding being enlightened, that we might know what is the hope of his calling, and what is the glory of *His inheritance* in the saints. (Ephesians 1:18)

May we die to self that he might inherit.

ABOUT THE AUTHOR

Theresa, who here is just calling herself the voice of one crying out in the wilderness, has been the wife of a pastor for many years and has also pastored alongside her husband.

She is the mother of two, grand-mother of two, and great-grand-mother of one. She is now retired and spends most of her time on the back side of the mountain, as she calls it, in spiritual warfare.

My desire for this book is to be a recruiter for the army of the Lord. Believing in the words of Deborah in Judges 5:23, "Curse says the angel of the Lord, the inhabitants thereof because they came not to the help of the Lord to the help of the Lord against the mighty."

The inhabitants of this world have not yet seen nor understood that we are in the most furious battle that this world will ever see. The enemies of the Lord are our enemies, and they know that they do not have much time left to foil the plans of God.

May God anoint and bless the ears of the hearers and enrich everyone with blessings from on high, strengthen their hands so that a bow of steel is broken by their arms, and make their feet like hinds' feet, able to stand strong and make progress on the high craggy places of trial and testing.

Sincerely and with love,

Theresa Holder